Demystifying Leadership Series:

10 Values of High Impact Leaders

MACK STORY

Make it happen!

Mack Story

DEDICATION

To the many people I have met along the way that have helped me grow as a person and as a leader. There have been many of you that have impacted me in ways you may never know.

I want to express special gratitude to those that were on the hundreds of cross-functional, Lean Kaizen event (continuous improvement) teams I have led over the years. You helped me sharpen, define, and refine my leadership skills through practical application. We also improved many processes together along the way.

We truly made a difference with others that wanted to make a difference with us!

CONTENTS

ACKNOWLEDGMENTS

I would like to acknowledge the late Dr. Stephen R. Covey, for writing, *The 7 Habits of Highly Effective People*, which provided my initial leadership insight and has been the foundation for my own personal transformation;

I would like to thank John C. Maxwell for mentoring me through his many books (especially *The 5 Levels of Leadership*), his endless inspiration and example, and his choice to leave his legacy through those of us he has certified as members of the John Maxwell Team.

INTRODUCTION

"There are leaders and there are those who lead. Leaders hold a position of power or influence. Those who lead us inspire us." ~ Simon Sinek

Leadership is Influence

Do you believe the person with the most influence, in any given situation, at any given time is the leader of the group? Notice, I didn't ask if the person with the most power, the highest rank, or the biggest title is the leader of the group. Think about the question deeply for a moment.

Forget all the questions that may be popping into your mind as you consider your answer. Keep your thoughts simple. If you have the most influence among a group of people, are you the leader of the group? Yes or no? Without a doubt, the person with the most influence is always the leader.

Do you believe you will be better off with more or less influence? Personally? Professionally? What would change in both areas if your influence increased?

My mentor, John Maxwell said it best, "Leadership is influence. Nothing more. Nothing less." The person with the most influence is the leader of the pack. As you read this book, understand the word influence can be used in place of the word leadership at any time. They are synonyms. Train yourself to use them interchangeably. But most importantly, when you speak with others, be sure to define leadership as influence to help them better understand they too are leaders, regardless of whether or not they have a formal position.

My belief that everything rises and falls on influence led me to write an entire book on influence, *Demystifying Leadership Series: Defining Influence* (I have included the *Defining Influence: Introduction* in the back of this book.). In *Defining Influence*, I help the reader discover many principles of influence and fully understand that everyone has influence. Therefore, based on my belief in John Maxwell's definition of influence, everyone is a leader.

The question is not, "Are you a leader?" But rather, "What kind of leader are you?" And most importantly, "What type of leader do you want to become?" How far do you want to grow?

Are you intentionally working to increase your influence? Should you be?

What would happen if your influence increased in every situation? Would your life be better? Would the life of those around you be better? Would you achieve better results? Would your income be more likely to increase? Would you have more options?

Increasing your influence always increases your options.

Consider the last time you were mad, sad, upset, or frustrated at home or at work. Was it because you had too much influence or not enough?

Consider a time when you needed help with a project and couldn't get it. Was it because you had too much influence or not enough?

I believe everything we ever achieve will be based on the amount of influence we have with others. However, I also believe in order to develop our influence with others, we first must influence ourselves. We must lead ourselves well before we can lead others well. If we want to lead better, we must be better. We must become higher level leaders than we are today.

"The future is in you now." ~ Terry A. Smith

People follow others for one of two reasons. They either "have to" or "want to." It's really that simple.

We don't want to be a low level leader others have to follow. We want to be more than the boss, the mom, or the dad. We want to build relationships and become high impact leaders others want to follow.

I remember something John Maxwell said in a lesson I heard him teach some time ago. He said, "There is a 40%

increase in productivity when comparing those that want to follow the leader with those that have to follow the leader." Wow! A 40% increase in productivity is amazing. I've witnessed plenty of this in my career and think the difference may actually be greater than 40%.

Pause and consider your work history and what you know about your friends and family members. Do most people report to someone they have to follow or want to follow? Do you hear them praising their boss or complaining about their boss?

A more important question to consider is, "Would you rather report to someone you have to follow or someone you want to follow?" If you have a formal position of authority, look down at those following you. Are they following you because they have to or because they want to?

If you have several or more people reporting to you, your relationship with each of them will be different. If you don't have a great relationship, they may follow you only because they have to; you're the boss. If you do have a great relationship with them, they want to, not because you're the boss, but because you have taken the time to build a solid relationship with them.

I believe people who love going to work and enjoy being with the people they work with and report to will, in fact, be 40% more productive if not more. What I know is people who follow someone only because they have to tend to only do what they have to do. You may have heard them say, "I'm just here to get a check." Or, "They don't pay me to think." Or, "It's not my job."

You can also rest assured the boss pays them the least possible to keep them on the job. Likewise, they are doing the least amount of work to keep a job. Everyone is losing.

When you hear those comments, you can be confident these people are following someone because they have to. What are they leaving on the table? How is poor leadership impacting their career? Their future? Their families? Their health?

However, when you hear someone say, "How can I help?" Or, "I know you only asked for this, but I thought it might be helpful if I went ahead and did a few more things too." Or, "Whatever it takes, I'll make it happen. You can count on me."

When you hear these comments, you know there is a strong and well developed relationship that serves as the foundation for the actions and thoughts of this person. These people are following because they want to. They are engaged in their job.

Over the last few decades, the focus has shifted from management to leadership to team leadership. To understand the difference, you must understand we *must* manage things and processes. Things and processes do not think. However, we should always lead people. People can think, and they do think. They do have an opinion, and they do want to express it. And, most importantly, they want to feel like their opinions and ideas matter. They truly want to be a part of the team.

"The guy who puts the ball through the hoop has ten hands." ~ John Wooden

The 10 Values

Our values are the foundation upon which we build our character. I'll be sharing 10 values high impact leaders work to master because they know these values will have a tremendous impact on their ability to lead others well. You may be thinking, "Aren't there more than 10 leadership values?" Absolutely! They seem to be endless. And, they are all important. These are simply 10 values I believe are key.

Since leadership is very dynamic, the more values you have been able to internalize and utilize synergistically together, the more effective you will be. The more influence you will have.

"High performing organizations that continuously invest in leadership development are now defining new 21st century leadership models to deal with today's gaps in their leadership pipelines and the new global business environment. These people-focused organizations have generated nearly 60% improved business growth, reported a 66% improvement in bench strength, and showed a 62% improvement in employee retention. And, our research shows that it is not enough to just spend money on leadership training, but rather to follow specific practices that drive accelerated business results." ~ Josh Bersin

Do you want to be a high impact leader?

I believe everyone is a leader, but they are leading at different levels.

I believe everyone can and should lead from *where they are*.

I believe everyone can and should make a high impact.

I believe growth doesn't just happen; we must make it happen.

I believe before you will invest in yourself you must first believe in yourself.

I believe leaders must believe in their team before they will invest in their team.

I truly believe *everything rises and falls on influence*.

There is a story of a tourist who paused for a rest in a small town in the mountains. He went over to an old man sitting on a bench in front of the only store in town and inquired, "Friend, can you tell me something this town is noted for?"

"Well," replied the old man, "I don't rightly know except it's the starting point to the world. You can start here and go anywhere you want."[1]

That's a great little story. We are all at "the starting point" to the world, and we "can start here and go anywhere we want." We can expand our influence 360° in all directions by starting in the center with ourselves.

Consider the illustration below. Imagine you are standing in the center. You can make a high impact. However, it will not happen by accident. You must become intentional. You must live with purpose while focusing on your performance as you develop your potential.

Why we do what we do is about our *purpose*.
How we do what we do is about our *performance*.
What we do will determine our *potential*.

Where these three components overlap, you will achieve a
HIGH IMPACT.

I hope you enjoy this journey discovering *10 Values of High Impact Leaders*. Let's get started.

1

THE VALUE OF VISION

Vision is the foundation of hope.

"When there's hope in the future, there's power in the present." ~ Les Brown

Vision begins with passion and ends with purpose. Vision is all about knowing where you're going.

When it comes to vision, our passion allows us to see more clearly short term. However, our purpose is what allows us to see clearly long term.

Do you like feeling stuck? Financially? Relationally? Personally? Professionally? I've never known anyone that enjoys that feeling.

Do you believe that to be where you are there was a time when you were uncomfortable? Personally? Professionally?

Do you believe a vision you developed in the past brought you to where you are today? Personally? Professionally?

When I talk to people about vision, they can usually reflect back to when they were working toward being where they are today. They understand without a vision on some level in the past, even if it was a low level vision, they would not be where they are today.

I believe a great vision begins with great passion. Without passion, we have very little vision. Our vision is mediocre at best. We must tap into our passion until we discover, uncover, define, and refine our purpose.

I believe the more intentional we are, relative to our personal growth, the more likely we are to always be growing toward our purpose. I believe this to be true for individuals and organizations. I believe we must follow our passion in order to find our purpose.

Too often, people who are searching in life find what they will settle for and stop looking for what they were searching for.

Unfortunately, many people will go to their grave never discovering their *why*. *Why* they are on this earth. Instead, they will choose to settle for mediocrity instead of greatness. Why would anyone settle for mediocrity when they could have greatness?

It's simple. It's easy to be mediocre, and it's hard to be great. It takes a lot of work to continually develop yourself, but it's worth the struggle to find your *why*.

> *"When we discover what we are willing to pay a price for, we discover our life's mission and purpose."*
> *~ Kevin Hall*

I believe vision is a byproduct of our growth. As we grow, we can see farther into the future. At the most basic level, growth can only occur when we change the way we think.

We must grow to develop our vision. The more we grow the greater our capacity to develop a clear, accurate, and achievable vision. Once we have grown enough to develop a clear vision, we must then grow toward our vision.

I believe transforming our vision into our reality is a byproduct of our discipline.

Discipline is the bridge between knowing (seeing the vision) and doing (transforming the vision into reality). It's a bridge we must cross every day. When we cross it, we move closer to realizing our dreams, but our vision is also projected farther at the same time. When we move forward, we can see farther.

As we grow, so grows our vision.

When we are not growing, there is no chance of moving beyond our current situation and circumstances. We are suffering from a self-imposed blindness and cannot see the possibilities the future holds for us. If we can't see it, we can't find it. If we can't find it, we won't benefit from it.

What we have done in the past has brought us to where we are today. If we were supposed to be someplace else, we would already be there. We are always exactly where we are supposed to be based on all of our previous growth. Our current way of thinking is just good enough to keep us in place assuming nothing externally changes.

But, we know everything around us is changing at an ever increasing pace. If we don't grow, adapt, and change, we will be left behind. In today's fast paced world, there is no such thing as sitting still. In life, we are either progressing or regressing. We must further develop our thinking if we want to increase our capacity to develop a vision beyond what we can currently see.

"The illiterate of the 21st century will not be those who cannot read and write but those who cannot learn, unlearn, and relearn." ~ Alvin Toffler

As we grow and develop our mind, we will begin to think differently. We will also begin to be different. We will begin to actually achieve more than we could have ever imagined in the past.

We will begin to develop the ability to imagine the potential for our lives farther into the future and see the potential that used to lie deep within us now rise to the surface as our reality. We will also begin to develop intuition in our areas of giftedness, where we have the most natural talents and abilities.

We may begin our personal growth journey for ourselves, but there will come a time when we will have grown so much our vision for ourselves begins to encompass others. If we believe in other people and we believe we have a responsibility to assist others on their journey, we will naturally gravitate towards those that want our help. As we grow ourselves, there will be a natural tendency to begin to help grow our organization, those within it, and those around us in our personal lives too.

"Every wise leader, whether a manager, a military officer, or a mother — should consider how to lead those who follow him or her as if inspiration were the only leadership leverage.

Good leaders inspire people. They breathe life into individuals and groups. They animate organizations. They breed the contagion of enthusiasm. They excite people to dream the dreams, take the risks, and make the sacrifices that are necessary to create better futures." ~ Terry A. Smith

High impact leadership begins with challenging yourself and ends with you having the desire and ability to effectively challenge others. Our true purpose is not success. It is to achieve significance as we help lift others. We cannot lift another without also lifting ourselves.

Success is about what we do for ourselves. Significance is about what we do for others.

Which person do you think will have more influence and have the ability to earn more during a lifetime?

- Someone who can't lead themselves well?
- Someone who demonstrates the ability to lead themselves well?
- Someone who can lead themselves and others well?

Being successful, and ultimately significant, is determined by your ability to influence others to achieve success at a high level.

Who would you rather follow? Someone with no vision that's happy with the status quo? Or, someone with a great vision that is constantly advancing themselves and others to a higher level? The answer is obvious: someone with great vision and the ability to turn their vision into reality.

If you want to lead at a high level, you must have a vision and aspire to transform it into reality through endless growth.

"A master in the art of living draws no sharp distinction between his work and his play; his labor and his leisure; his mind and his body: his education and his recreation. He hardly knows which is which. He simply pursues his vision of excellence through whatever he is doing, and leaves others to determine whether he is working or playing. To himself, he is always doing both." ~ L. P. Jacks

Transformation Turns Vision into Reality

Where will you have the greatest influence? You will discover you have the greatest influence in the area where you also have the greatest passion. What motivates and inspires you will give you the energy and authenticity to motivate and inspire others.

"You will not grow without attempting things you are unable to do." ~ Dr. Henry Cloud

In order to fully leverage your passion to increase your influence, you must use it to find, reveal, and refine your *why* – your purpose.

Discovering your purpose doesn't happen accidentally as you go through life. It happens intentionally as you grow through life. Once you discover your purpose, you do not stop. You cannot stop. You focus on it for the rest of your life as you begin to live life on purpose for a purpose.

Every day you allow your passion to fuel your growth is a day you discover more and learn more about your purpose. When your vision flows from your passion and purpose, you find clarity and become highly effective and highly influential. Play becomes work, and work becomes play. For these lucky few, they are able to trade in their two day weekend for a seven day weekend.

The 10 Foundational Elements of Transformation

1. Thought is the Foundation of Choice

If you already knew what you needed to know, you would already be where you want to go. Until we change what we think, we will not change what we do. Our thoughts are only real to us. No one else is aware of them. They can and do lead to other private thoughts. However, they only become known to others when they lead us into conscious action, when we make a physical choice. When we act, our thoughts are translated to the world as choices, and who we are on the inside is revealed on the outside.

The Choice Formula:

Thought + Emotion + Action = Choice

Thought – something we are consciously aware of in our mind

Emotion – something we subconsciously feel based on our thoughts

Action – something we do based on our thoughts and emotions

"The outer world of circumstance shapes itself to the inner world of thought." ~ James Allen

2. Choice is the Foundation of Vision

Developing a vision, big or small, is a choice. We must think on purpose about our purpose. There is no conscious action without conscious thought. When it comes to creating a vision for ourselves, our life, our team, or our organization, we must intentionally tap into our passion and purpose to begin to think of what could be. We can turn our potential into our reality. The quality of our choices depends on the quality of our thoughts.

At this level, we choose to dream of what is possible. We let our imagination run wild. What do we want to be? Who do we want to become? Where do we want to go? We don't ask, "Can we do it?" We ask, "What is possible?" An effective vision taps into our strengths not our weaknesses. We will have the greatest impact and receive the greatest reward when we stay in our strength zone.

"Vision is not enough. It must be combined with venture. It is not enough to stare up the steps; we must step up the stairs." ~ Vaclav Havel

3. Vision is the Foundation of Hope

Several years ago, I discovered a rather odd but impactful story about the power of hope. I was amazed by it! In it, an experiment was being performed with laboratory rats to measure their motivation to live under different circumstances.

Scientists dropped a rat into a jar of water that had been placed in total darkness (no vision), and they timed how long the animal would continue swimming before it gave up hope and allowed itself to drown. They found the rat usually lasted little more than three minutes without hope. Then, they dropped another rat into the same kind of jar, but instead of placing it in total darkness, they allowed a ray of light (hope) to shine into it.[1]

Under those circumstances, the rat kept swimming for 36 hours!

That's 720 times longer than the one in the dark without hope!

Because the rat could see (vision), it continued to have hope. If that is true for a rat, imagine the amount of hope a strong and powerful personal vision will provide to each of us. We are much more capable of imagining and reasoning ourselves into a brighter future, one filled with light instead of darkness.

Once we have a clearly defined vision, we must again ask ourselves, "Is it possible my vision could become my reality?" We should also seek reinforcement from those around us that believe in us and our mission. Without hope, our vision will fade into darkness just as it did with the rat. But with hope, the light continues to shine brightly on our vision giving us a reason to "keep swimming." We must maintain hope that our vision will become our reality.

Knowing it is in fact possible will give us hope. Having faith in the vision will give us hope. Having people believe in us and our vision will give us hope. Knowing others have done what we want to do will give us hope.

Hope is not a strategy. However, hope is necessary to develop a strategy. Why? Without hope, you won't develop a strategy. Without hope, your vision is doomed. Without hope, you will remain bound.

"Where there is no belief or hope for growth to be real, it is no longer attempted. People, or organizations, enter into a state of sameness, and as we have seen, that is really when things are no longer alive. Death is taking over not growth."
~ Dr. Henry Cloud

4. Hope is the Foundation of Sacrifice

Without hope, there will be no sacrifice. If we don't believe strongly enough in ourselves and our vision, we will not have the strength or desire to make the sacrifices needed to transform our vision into our reality. We are exactly where we are supposed to be based on our choices and the sacrifices we've made leading up to today. If we want to move closer to our vision, we must make different choices and additional sacrifices. Sacrifice is giving up something of lesser value now for something of greater value later.

Why is sacrifice so hard? Because we feel the loss immediately. However, we may not feel the gain for days, weeks, months, or even years. When we begin to discover our purpose, we will also begin to value some things more than others. Then, those things of lesser value holding us back will begin to naturally drop away. We must give up to go up. Then, we must give up even more to stay up. But ultimately, we must give up even more if we want to go up more.

It's like fitness. You must give up to get fit. You have to continue to give up to stay fit. And, if you want to go to a higher level of fitness, you must give up even more.

"Men and women who have accomplished much have sacrificed much. Nothing given – nothing received. No weeping – no reaping."
~ John C. Maxwell

5. Sacrifice is the Foundation of Discipline

Unfortunately, sacrifice alone will not convert your vision into reality. When we sacrifice, we remove things from our life that are holding us back. We rid ourselves of those things that are tapping into our resources such as time, money, and energy. Recovering some of our most valuable resources is only half the battle. Now that we have made additional resources available, we must intentionally use them to advance toward our vision.

We must develop self-discipline. As we progress from knowing and begin doing, we are crossing the bridge called discipline. Crossing this bridge allows us to begin turning our goals, dreams, and vision into reality. Discipline is giving ourselves a command and following through with it.

We must do the right thing for the right reason at the right time if we are going to be effective.

"If you do what is easy, your life will be hard. But if you do what is hard, your life will be easy."
~ Les Brown

6. Discipline is the Foundation of Growth

As we develop discipline, we begin to grow toward our vision. The more discipline we have the more growth we will achieve. When we take the right steps toward our vision, discipline allows us to convert our sacrifices into growth. Growth is about reaching and stretching. John Maxwell often speaks about the Law of the Rubber Band. He says, "People are like rubber bands, we are only adding value when we are being stretched."

Often, what we are reaching for can only be obtained by letting go of something we have been holding on to.

Growth doesn't just happen. It doesn't simply come with age. If it did, all of the older people would be more successful than all of the younger people. That's just not how it works. We must make a choice to be intentional about growth.

I'll refer back to the fitness example. We do not become fit accidentally. Likewise, we will not grow accidentally. We must develop an intentional growth plan we know will move us toward our vision. You should also know you can change without growing, but you cannot grow without changing.

"Growth is painful. Change is painful. But, nothing is as painful as being stuck somewhere you don't belong." ~ Zig Ziglar

7. Growth is the Foundation of Change

Overall, we will be more effective if we stay growth oriented instead of goal oriented. That does not mean we do not set goals. Sure we do. We should always set goals that support our continuous growth. Keep in mind, the goal of growth is not change for the sake of change. The goal of growth is positive change. What determines if the change is positive? It keeps moving you closer to your vision.

Where will you see the most benefit when your growth leads to change? Character growth will always produce the greatest results because it acts like a multiplier relative to your competency. You will see the most positive change when you work in areas of weakness relative to your character.

The second area where your growth will show up is in your competency. However, when working to create positive change relative to your competency, you should always work in areas of strength where you are naturally gifted. Character will take you most of the way, and competency will take you the rest of the way.

"When we are faced with change, we either step forward into growth or we step backward into safety." ~ Abraham Maslow

8. Change is the Foundation of Success

Without change, there can be no improvement. But beware, just because you change doesn't mean you will become successful. You must change the right things for the right reasons. If you truly want success, don't focus on becoming successful. Focus first on becoming more valuable. As you become more valuable, you will become more successful. The most valuable people are also the most successful people.

If you'll develop the habits of success, you'll make success a habit. Successful people invest time and money to grow and develop themselves because *they* value themselves and know this truth: life **IS** hard! So, they take responsibility for making it a little easier.

Success is all about you and what you have achieved.

However, to make a high impact, you must shift your focus to significance which is all about helping others become successful. Significance is not about how far we advance ourselves but how far we advance others.

> *"Before you are a leader, success is all about growing yourself. When you become a leader, success is all about growing others." ~ Jack Welch*

9. Success is the Foundation of Significance

High impact leaders do not stop at success. They hunger for more. Not for themselves, but for others. They understand success is just a stepping stone along the path toward significance. When I was training leaders in Guatemala with John Maxwell in 2013, I remember John saying, "Once you have tasted significance, nothing else will satisfy you." That trip to Guatemala was life changing for many of us. We went there to give to others, but we received much more than we gave.

With significance, what started out as a simple vision for your own personal growth has now compounded into a vision to help others achieve and succeed. You no longer have to sacrifice for yourself. You have already succeeded. But, if you want to taste significance, you now must sacrifice for the benefit of others.

Most won't do it. But, the few that do will move far beyond success to achieve a life of significance. Those that have achieved significance will leave a legacy through the success of others.

"You and I live in an age when only a rare minority of individuals desire to spend their lives in pursuit of objectives which are bigger than they are. In our age, for most people, when they die it will be as though they never lived."
~ Rusty Rustenbach

10. Significance is the Foundation of Legacy

When you choose a life of significance, your life is no longer just about you and what you have accomplished. It's far bigger than any one individual. It's about touching the lives of others in a way that what you leave in them flows into others. When you achieve significance your influence is multiplied through others. Significance is not about you, but it starts with you.

Your legacy will not be defined by what you leave behind *for* others. It will be defined by what you leave behind *within* others. What will determine if your vision becomes your legacy? It won't be you. It will be those that felt valued by you. It will be those that were able to allow your influence to pass through them into the lives of others.

"The things you do for yourself are gone when you are gone, but the things you do for others remain as your legacy." ~ Kalu Ndukwe Kalu

2

THE VALUE OF MODELING

Someone is always watching you.

"Who we are on the inside is what people see on the outside." ~ Mack Story

Who is watching you? A lot more people than you realize. They are watching at home, at work, at church, at dinner, at your child's sporting event, as you shop, as you drive along the highway, and every other place you go where other people are. You are being watched non-stop.

I can't write about the *value of modeling* without mentioning a humorous story I came across some time ago.

A mother and her adult daughter were out shopping one day, trying to make the most of a big sale weekend before Christmas. As they went from store to store in the mall, the older woman complained about everything; the crowds, the poor quality of the merchandise, the prices, and her sore feet.

After the mother experienced a particularly difficult interaction with a clerk in one department store, she turned to her daughter and said, "I'm never going back to that store again. Did you see the dirty look she gave me?"

The daughter answered, "She didn't give it to you, Mom. You had it when you went in!"[1]

I'm sure the daughter wasn't the only one that had noticed the mother throughout the day. Many others were watching too. What did they see? How did it affect their opinion of her? Do you think her influence increased or decreased with the people she met that day?

Why does it even matter? Does it matter? Absolutely! It matters, and it matters a lot. What about those saying, "I don't care what others think about me." They are free not to care, but that doesn't stop other people from thinking what they think based on what they see.

Who's watching us is important, but what they see is the most important. When we interact with other people, we are always doing one of two things. We are either building trust or creating distrust. Not sometime. Every time.

Not just with those we are talking to, but also with anyone watching us. And, someone is always watching. When it comes to those watching us, we are either increasing our influence with them or decreasing it. Which one we do is based on our choices. Ultimately, our choices make us who we are.

Your choices will make you or break you. Think about it. I bet at some point in your life you have seen someone interact with another person and their interaction caused you to distrust them although they had never even spoken a word to you. Sometimes, someone can simply walk through a door, and the instant we see them we don't trust them because of what they look like, what they do, how they do it, when they do it, who they do it with, how they dress, or their body language.

What people see matters. And, it matters a lot.

"What we say accounts for only 7% of what is believed. The way we say it accounts for 38%. But, what others see accounts for 55%!" ~ John C. Maxwell

Modeling is my absolute favorite value. Why? Because this value reveals how we're doing on all the others. What everyone sees on the outside is what we truly are on the inside.

We can hide what we think, but we can't hide who we are.

I'm going to share a few personal and business related stories to illustrate the principle associated with modeling.

First, I want to share a related quote that's been at the top of my list since I first heard it. My son, Eric, shared it with me.

He saw it on a picture hanging in the hallway of a school where he was making a sales call. He thought I would like it, so he took a picture with his phone and sent it to me.

He was right. I loved it! I'm also very grateful he thought of me when he read it. With people, the little things are the big things. When you read this quote, pause and think deeply about the meaning of the words.

"If we are not modeling what we're teaching, then we are teaching something else." ~ Abraham Maslow

There is so much truth in these words. To put it a different way, we are not always teaching what we are teaching. But, we *are* always teaching what we are modeling.

We don't teach what we say. We teach what we do, which is simply a reflection of who we are.

Others don't learn much from our words. However, they learn a lot from our actions. Far too often, what comes out of a person's mouth isn't what comes out of their heart. What comes out of their mouth may or may not be the truth. But, what comes out of their heart (their actions) is always truth. It's all about who they are, not who they think they are.

Think about this: Are you in the modeling business?

I believe we all are. Let me tell you why.

In June 2013, my wife Ria and I had the privilege to join John Maxwell in Guatemala City, Guatemala as he initiated the "Transformation Begins with Me!" cultural transformation. We joined John and 150 other John Maxwell Team coaches to train more than 20,000 Guatemalan leaders in just under three days. All of us were invited to participate in a national television broadcast with the President of Guatemala at the Presidential Palace. He was casting his vision of transformation on live TV to the Guatemalan people. We created some amazing memories and met some amazing people too.

One of those people was my interpreter, Bertha. Since most people there spoke Spanish and most of us only spoke English, the majority of us needed interpreters.

On the first day of training, Bertha and I were assigned to train approximately 50 high level business leaders together. She was awesome at just 20 years old! While in the taxi on our way there, we talked and got to learn a little about each other. As usual, I was teaching leadership values whenever there was an opportunity. I also wanted her to understand I saw her as much more than "just an interpreter."

I wanted her to know I saw her as a young leader with a big role to play in the transformation of Guatemala.

As we walked into the room to get setup, something I had said caused her to share a thought I had triggered in her. Bertha looked at me and said, "I don't know if I want to be a role model Mack." I tilted my head a little and looked at her sincerely and said, "Bertha you already are because someone is always watching you. The real question is not, 'Do you want to be a role model?' but rather, 'What kind of role model will you be?'"

I could tell she was in deep thought for several minutes after my comments. I knew she was considering the principle behind modeling. We talked more about this later when we had a chance. I wanted to be sure she understood we influence other people through our actions whether we intend to or not. We may never know how or when our actions have influenced others or if our influence was positive or negative.

I share the story of Bertha often when speaking on leadership. It's always interesting to see how the story impacts those in the audience. Many of them have the same look Bertha had when I spoke those words to her. Many haven't really thought about it before.

At the end of my smaller training sessions, I often leave time for each person to share what was most impactful to them. Recently, I was conducting a leadership session with a group of 26 team members from an electrical construction company. When I was finished, I had intentionally left enough time available for each person to speak.

This is always the best part of the session for me. I get to hear, see, and feel the impact of my words.

As we went around the room, one gentleman said, "One thing I got out of this training session is that I've got to pay more attention to the example I'm setting (*Value of Modeling*). I have a 6 year old, and I've noticed many of the things I say are starting to come out of his mouth. And, I don't like it. I need to change who I am and what I do." This gentleman got it. It's not the child's fault. He (the leader) is responsible.

During the class, I had shared the following story with them about one of my many failures, as a father, to be a good leader. I was referencing a time earlier in my life when I got it wrong. At the time, I didn't know what I didn't know. I wasn't being a positive model for anyone, much less my son. Here is what I shared that day that made the impact.

I chose to quit drinking alcohol in May 2012 and also stopped using all profanity soon after. I had personally applied the leadership principles I teach and had grown to a point I no longer valued it. It wasn't serving my purpose any longer. I no longer want it, and I've never missed it. I haven't had a drop of alcohol since I made the decision to stop and will never have another drop. Alcohol is no longer a part of who I am.

"Good character is more to be praised than outstanding talent. Most talents are, to some extent, a gift. Good character, by contrast, is not given to us. We have to build it piece by piece: by thought, choice, courage, and determination." ~ John Luther

However, from age 15-42 (I'll be 46 in August 2015.), I drank alcohol fairly often, not daily, usually just on the weekends. I made a lot of other dumb choices while I was drinking and having a "good time" with my like-minded friends too. We did some really stupid things!

Although, for many of the early years, I intentionally didn't use alcohol around Eric at all. As he got older, I seemed to care less for some reason. My best guess is because he could take care of himself as he got older without being fully dependent upon me any longer.

For many years, until Eric was 20, I had modeled that I valued alcohol. As I sit and write these words, I think of how poor of an example as a leader (father) I was for him in this area. Knowing what I know today, I was absolutely a terrible example. At the time, I didn't have a clue. And like most parents that drink alcohol, I encouraged him *not* to do it while I was *doing it* myself. There's definitely something wrong with that picture.

I also shared with the class that neither of my parents ever drank in our home. If they ever drank at all while I lived with them, I never knew it. As far as I know, they didn't. However, that didn't stop me from doing it. They modeled a good example. They can rest assured I didn't start drinking because they did.

I don't have that option. Because I drank alcohol around Eric, I don't know. He started drinking at an early age like me. Although I was still drinking, I didn't like that he was. I didn't want him to do it. I wanted him to be better than me.

I'll never truly know if he started drinking because of me. But what I do know is that his liquor of choice happens to be the one I liked the most. I'm not proud to be sharing this with you. It's simply the truth. I share it with you to help illustrate the *Value of Modeling*. Who we are matters because someone's always watching.

I hope and pray the positive example I'm modeling today will influence him as he grows older. I have positively influenced him in many other ways. I am proud of that. I also don't beat myself up over what happened in the past. It's in my circle of concern. I have no influence or control over it now.

What I can do is look backward and use the lessons to move forward more effectively and help others learn from my past mistakes by being transparent.

I can look back at my past, pull out the lessons, learn from them, and teach them to others. When the gentleman shared his story in class, it affirmed the value of sharing mine as I often do. I'm very open and tend to talk about my past choices and personal struggles when speaking on leadership.

> *"We are anxious to improve our circumstances but unwilling to improve ourselves. We therefore remain bound." ~ James Allen*

I've done a lot of work on myself to be where I am today. I'm in a really good place on many fronts. I continue to invest my time and money to grow myself and use my knowledge, skills, and experiences to help others avoid some of the pitfalls I've had in the past. I've had great success and have helped a lot of people along the way. It's always a great feeling to know I've made a positive impact.

My goal is to accelerate the growth of others by helping them to move from where they are personally and professionally to where they want to be. The farther you climb up the leadership (influence) ladder, the narrower the gap will be between your personal and professional life. If you want to keep climbing, you've got to close the gap. You've got to be one whole person, not one person at work and another away from work.

As I told the group in the recent training session, "Your cumulative influence in life is based on who you are 24 hours a day, 7 days a week, 365 days a year."

Who you are outside of work has a huge impact on the amount of influence you have at work. If you don't understand this, you have work to do because you don't know what you don't know and are lower on the leadership scale than you may think. If you do understand, you are already at a much higher level than most people will ever reach.

You must be more before others can see more.

They see us for who we are not who we want to be. Who we are is also who we attract. The only people that will buy the "picture" we paint are those that like what they see. Those that value what we value and believe what we believe. Otherwise, they're not interested.

You can't raise the bar for others if you can't reach it yourself.

3

THE VALUE OF RESPONSIBILITY

When we take responsibility, we take control.

"What is common sense is not always common practice." ~ Dr. Stephen R. Covey

Would you like to learn the secret to climbing the ladder of success efficiently and effectively?

Why should you listen to me?

What qualifies me to write this lesson? My life. My personal transformation that's a direct result of me applying the principles I write and speak about. I have applied what I'm going to share with you since joining the U.S. Marine Corps Reserve as an 0311 Infantryman at age 18 in 1987 and accepting my first job as an entry-level machine operator in a hot, dirty manufacturing facility in 1988. Today, I often train and consult with top leaders and business owners, their leadership teams, and positional level leaders at every other level. I very much enjoy the privilege of growing and developing entry-level team members too when given the opportunity.

What do I use to validate this lesson? My results. I share my story with humility and integrity to support and validate the principles found in this lesson, not with pride and ego. Without knowing my actual results, this would be an empty leadership lesson. However, I want my words to have meaning. I want my words to improve your effectiveness and positively impact your success.

As I write these words, my hourly rates have risen to many hundreds of times what they were when I started out in 1988. They continue to rise as they always have since those early days of being an entry-level machine operator that barely graduated high school.

It's not about becoming successful. It's about becoming valuable.

"From the neck down, we are worth about $10 hour.
From the neck up, we are priceless."
~ Harvard Business Review

I don't write this to impress you. I have no need to impress you. However, I do want to impress upon you that no matter where you are, you can be more, do more, and have more.

I grew up in Tallassee, Alabama, a small town of less than 6,000 people. Neither of my parents graduated high school. I barely graduated myself. I have an uncommon story that has also allowed me to achieve uncommon results.

What is the secret that has allowed me, an entry-level, blue-collar factory worker, to climb the corporate ladder and eventually become successfully self-employed as an International Leadership Development Trainer, Coach, Speaker and Lean Manufacturing Consultant earning hourly rates that I could have never even imagined as I began my career?

Warning: The secret says easy, but it does hard.

The Secret

Here's the secret to climbing the ladder of success and increasing your value: Don't ask for a raise or a promotion. Ask for more responsibility.

Then, deliver. If you can't deliver, you have character work to do. If you don't want to ask for responsibility without first receiving a raise or a promotion, you have character work to do. *To grow professionally, you must grow personally.* As I continue to teach this principle here, I'm assuming personal growth and character development are already a habit for you. If not, please consider reading my book, *Defining Influence.*

Whenever I teach this lesson in my leadership development seminars, I always tell the audience to get their pen and paper ready because I'm going to share a secret that will continuously take their career to new heights, *if they're willing to make it a habit.*

"We are what we repeatedly do. Excellence, then, is not an act, but a habit." ~ Aristotle

Once I have their attention, I start by saying, "Okay. I want everyone to write this down because it will work. I know. I have done it and continue to do it. Here it is. If you want to climb the ladder of success and increase your pay throughout your career…" Everyone starts writing because they are fully engaged and want to capture the secret. So, I pause for a moment and let them catch up. Then, I continue, "….don't ask for a raise or a promotion. Ask for more responsibility."

Something interesting always happens when they hear me say, "Ask for more responsibility." Many of them stop writing and look up at me. It literally stops some of them in their tracks. They're either questioning and unsure if they're buying into it, or they already know they don't want to ask for more responsibility.

Either way, those pausing are instantly skeptical and don't want to write it down, much less do it! I re-engage them by saying, "I know it's not what you expected. But, write it down. If you want to grow and go, don't ask for more money. Ask for more responsibility. Trust me. Write it down."

"The successful person has the habit of doing the things failures don't like to do." ~ E.M. Gray

Responsibility Pays

If you will make a habit of asking for and accepting more responsibility, you will climb the ladder of success and your value to others will increase (assuming you have done the necessary work on your character development to get to the next level). However, you must understand the company where you are currently working may not be the one to give you a raise or even promote you. They should be the one to reward you, but often, it's another company that will place a higher value on you. Then, if you are willing to go in order to grow, you will achieve your goal and reap the rewards of applying the principle of asking for more responsibility.

As I've already mentioned, if you want become a success, do not focus on becoming more successful. Focus on becoming more valuable. Who would be more valuable on your team? Someone asking for more responsibility or someone transferring more responsibility?

When you ask for and embrace more responsibility, you will always become more valuable. Not only to the company where you are working, but also to other companies that value the knowledge and experience you have gained along the way. Those that value who you are, what you know, and what you can do will be happy to offer you an appropriate salary and a position.

Something to Consider

You're the boss. You have the ability to give one person a raise and/or promotion, but there are two eligible. Both are outstanding and amazing team members. One is constantly asking for more money. The other is constantly asking for more responsibility. You're the boss. Who gets the raise? Most people don't hesitate so say, "The one asking for more responsibility."

Or, consider a much different scenario. Times are tough and economic conditions are bad. You must make a tough decision and terminate one of them. Which one will you keep? Again, most people don't hesitate to say, "The one asking for more responsibility."

A Real-Life Example

I could share endless examples from my 25+ year journey of growth applying the *Value of Responsibility*. The personal story I will share next illustrates what the principle looks like when practiced. (If you want more details on my personal journey and my professional transformation, I've captured much of it in my book, *Defining Influence*. It's available at amazon.com or for a signed copy, go to mackstory.com.)

In 1997, I had been steadily advancing in my manufacturing career. I was a machine setup technician on the night shift responsible for knowing how to operate and setup nearly all of the 70 or so CNC (computer numerical control) machines throughout the entire manufacturing facility. Considering I had started my career in 1988 with the responsibility for only one very simple machine, I had already stepped up and asked for additional responsibility many times in my career.

Nine years into my career, and I had already made asking for more responsibility a habit. Now, it was time to do it again.

A new work cell had been added with several machines (a twin spindle lathe, a gear shaper, and a vertical milling center). It was critical to operations and was being operated by someone that had many years of experience in the company, much more than me. But, there was a problem.

After nearly a year with the veteran in charge of this new cell, output was still much less than had been anticipated. The senior operator continuously gave negative feedback concerning the work cell. I remember him most often complaining, "It'll never work. It's too much for one person to do. What were *they* thinking?" I'm sure you can understand, with this attitude, he insured it would never work.

He didn't want to do what was right. He wanted to be right.

After a year, he had decided to seek another job in the plant. He was tired of operating this work cell and was constantly in conflict with those truly responsible for making it work: his supervisor and those in the engineering department. In other words, he was tired of banging his head against the wall and getting nowhere.

He wasn't going to take responsibility for making it work. He was going to transfer it to someone else.

When I heard this work cell would be open on the day shift, I was excited to apply for it. During my interview, I said I believed I could help bring the output up to expectations and would love the responsibility and the challenge of doing so. I was basically jumping up and shouting, "Pick me! I can and will make it happen!!"

They did pick me. Now, it was time to make it happen!

I didn't ask for a raise. I also didn't get a raise. But, I did ask for responsibility, and I got that. I got the job. I also know what comes after you accept and master the responsibility you've asked for: a raise and a promotion will also be in your future. I've done it over and over and over again. I'm still doing it and will never stop doing it. It works!

At the time, I was a machine operator. I wasn't a machine programmer. Without being told what to do or how to do it, I accepted responsibility for improving the cell's output. I immediately started capturing the cycle time at each machine for every item produced in the work cell. I created a spreadsheet, so I could pick up where I left off the last time a particular item was produced.

Then, I started figuring out how to improve the slowest cycle (bottleneck) of each item knowing I couldn't produce any faster than the slowest machine in the process. I repeated this process daily for months.

As a result, I was responsible for doubling the output of the work cell, a 100% increase in productivity in just six months. I had not complained, but I had taken initiative, simplified, and improved the process. Not only could I operate the work cell at this level, but also the operators on the other shifts could too.

I never said it wouldn't work. I took responsibility and made it work. After earning a raise, I got a raise. But, I never asked for a raise. I didn't have to.

My actions not only made me more successful, but also those on other shifts, the supervisors and engineers shared in the success. Ultimately, the organization as a whole was more profitable. The whole team was better, not just me.

Unexpected Opportunity

My results also led me to an unforeseen opportunity a few months later. Unforeseen opportunities are the byproduct of asking for more responsibility.

A highly sought after CNC programming position opened up unexpectedly. There were only two positions to support the entire facility which had approximately 70 different types and brands of machines. When a position opened up, there were always a lot of applicants. Typically, the most senior operators had the best chance because they had the most experience. However, this time things were different.

"The secret to success in life is for a man to be ready for his time when it comes." ~ Benjamin Disraeli

As I had worked to improve the machine cycle times on all of the items produced in the work cell, I also had learned A LOT about CNC programming. In the beginning, I didn't have a clue about programming. After six months, I could rewrite the programs and make the necessary edits without assistance. I had learned to program the machines while only being required to operate the machines. Programming wasn't my responsibility, but I made it my responsibility. I didn't just come in and push the buttons every day as required.

I came in and did more than was required. I did things before they were required. And, I did things better than was required. When the programming job opened up, I applied and was selected to fill the position. Had I not taken on more responsibility as an operator, I would not have been qualified.

Just like last time, in the interview process, I didn't ask for more money, I only asked for more responsibility. This time, however, I got more responsibility, more money, and a promotion. But most importantly, I got the opportunity to repeat the cycle as I had already learned to do. Amazing results and growth always followed.

"If it's meant to be, it's up to me." ~ Truett Cathy

This story is symbolic of my entire career. Sometimes, I got the raise in the organization where I learned and made the improvements. Sometimes, I got the raise when I accepted a new challenge at a new organization based on my results at the previous organization. I always consistently got the raise as I continued to climb the ladder of success and accepted more responsibility.

Think about it. When someone starts a new job, they do not receive their pay check on the first day. They typically must do the work (usually one or two weeks). Then, they are paid for the work they have already done. Life is no different.

Asking for responsibility instead of a raise is much the same. Perform first, and then, get promoted and paid second. As I mentioned early on in this lesson, character is the key. If you have the competency to do more but are not being given the opportunity, take a look in the mirror. The face we see least is our own.

Your character may be holding you back. Meaning, your boss doesn't think you are deserving based on character not competency. Or, your character may be holding you in place. Meaning, you are unwilling to make the changes and take the risks to move to another department or organization where you could excel. In either case, the problem is not the boss. The problem is always within us. We are always responsible.

This reminds me of one of my favorite stories I've heard John Maxwell tell many times about taking or should I say avoiding responsibility.

A man in a hot air balloon realized he was lost. He reduced altitude and spotted a woman below. He descended a bit more and shouted, "Excuse me, can you help me? I promised a friend I would meet him an hour ago, but I don't know where I am."

The woman below replied, "You're in a hot air balloon hovering approximately 30 feet above the ground. You're between 40 and 41 degrees north latitude and between 59 and 60 degrees west longitude."

"You must be an engineer," said the balloonist. "I am," replied the woman, "How did you know?"

"Well," answered the balloonist, "everything you told me is, technically correct, but I've no idea what to make of your information, and the fact is I'm still lost.

Frankly, you've not been much help at all. If anything, you've delayed my trip."

The woman below responded, "You must be in Management."

"I am," replied the balloonist, "but how did you know?"

"Well," said the woman, "you don't know where you are or where you're going. You have risen to where you are due to a large quantity of hot air. You made a promise which you've no idea how to keep, and you expect people beneath you to solve your problems. The fact is you are in exactly the same position you were in before we met, but now, somehow, it's my fault."

Not only did the balloonist avoid responsibility for the situation he found himself in, but he also immediately started to transfer the responsibility at his first opportunity. Dr. Henry Cloud basically put it this way in one of his recent articles on blame when he said, "Blame is comfort food for the soul."

Our character development is the biggest obstacle along our career path. Many people spend years working on their competency gaining experience and earning degrees. But, the majority spend very little time intentionally working on their character development.

If we want to change our circumstances and results, we must change the way we think.

"Where success is concerned, people are not measured in inches, or pounds, or college degrees, or family background; they are measured by the size of their thinking. How big we think determines the size of our accomplishments." ~ David Schwartz

4

THE VALUE OF TIMING

It matters when you do what you do.

"It's about doing the right thing for the right reason at the right time." ~ Mack Story

Have you considered the effect timing has on your leadership (influence)? If not, you need to know it's huge!

High impact leaders know another secret: timing can be used to leverage influence. Because of this inside knowledge, they are methodical, intentional, and most of all, patient. They will always wait for the right time to do the right thing for the right reason.

John C. Maxwell said it this way:

- *The wrong action at the wrong time leads to disaster.*
- *The right action at the wrong time brings resistance.*
- *The wrong action at the right time is a mistake.*
- *The right action at the right time results in success.*

Timing is very difficult to teach and equally difficult to learn. First, you must become aware of the power of timing. Next, you must reflect intentionally in order to better understand what happened and the impact timing had on the outcome.

Timing can turn something you say or do into a positive, motivating interaction with your team, increasing your influence with them. Or, timing can turn something you say or do into a negative, demoralizing interaction with your team, decreasing your influence with them.

Our understanding of the use of timing is very closely related to our intuition. Let's look at a few examples of how timing effects our results. These examples will help you better understand the *Value of Timing*. When you read them, try and think of areas where you are naturally good when it comes to timing and intuition and areas where you're not so good.

When it comes to timing, we excel in areas of our natural giftedness: those things we do with ease that others do with stress.

If someone excels in the area of cooking, they may not need a timer at all. They are so tuned in to the smell, the look, the taste, even the feel when stirring, they don't need a timer to know when it's ready. Timing is not holding them back at all. They have a natural instinct or intuition when it comes to cooking.

Cooking is not my gift. I hate to cook. If I was going to prepare a dish, I would definitely need a timer along with detailed instructions. And, I still wouldn't get it right because I would be thinking too much about everything else. My conscious mind would be overloaded with the entire experience. I would probably even forget to set the timer!

However, put me on a mountain bike on a technical trail twisting and turning through a forest filled with rocks, roots, step descents, drop offs, loose soil, and you'll see my natural intuition and timing on full display. I love it, and I'm good at it. I seldom crash although it does happen to the best of us from time to time.

I've been mountain biking consistently since 2008, several thousand miles per year at times, over all kinds of terrain in all kinds of conditions. My subconscious mind is now processing much of what I had to consciously think about and process in the past. There's no way my conscious mind could process all of the different variables at full speed. My timing would be way off.

Someone recently asked me, "How often do you crash?" After thinking about it for a bit, I could only remember three serious crashes over the last seven years. I was only injured during one (separated shoulder & concussion). There may have been other small mishaps too. If I can't remember it, it wasn't what I would call a real crash. However, the opportunity to crash is there every time I ride. (It's the same with leadership too!) I hope crash number four isn't too bad. It's been a while, so odds are it's going to be sooner rather than later.

Why is it easier for me to ride a mountain bike than to cook? On the surface, it doesn't really make sense. Cooking is much easier, right? Not for me! I don't possess the foundational element needed to be a great cook: a passion for cooking. I'm not interested or committed.

"When you're interested in something, you do it only when it's convenient. But, when you're committed to something, you accept no excuses, only results."
~ Ken Blanchard

Generally speaking, mountain biking is obviously much more challenging and difficult than cooking. The reason I can ride a mountain bike much better than I can cook is that I have an interest, natural talents, and abilities in the areas related to riding a bicycle off-road such as balance and hand/eye coordination. All of that alone isn't enough, I have intentionally continued to develop my skills in the area of mountain biking by pedaling thousands of miles on many different trails. As a result, my subconscious now does most of the work for me. I hardly even have to think any more. I just pedal.

When it comes to leadership (influencing people), the more we know subconsciously, the better we will lead.

Influence is another area in which I also have a natural gift. Beyond understanding why and how the many principles of influence build trust, inspire, and motivate people to action,

I also fully understand the importance of timing related to influence.

> *"Trust your hunches. They're usually based on facts filed away just below the conscious level."*
> ~ *Joyce Brothers*

Far too many leaders either don't understand timing, or worse, don't care. I can always help those that don't understand. They just need more exposure to the principles and a deeper understanding of how the many principles of influence are connected. My passion and purpose is to help others increase their positive influence.

When someone simply doesn't care about increasing their influence, much less improving their timing, there's not much chance of them changing for the better. The number one reason they don't care is they are satisfied with the influence that comes with their position. In their mind, waiting for the right time slows them down.

On the leadership scale, they are very low level leaders. They are satisfied with their level of influence. They rely on their position to influence others, not their character.

For a high impact leader, timing is an issue when it comes to dealing with these low level leaders that don't care about learning the principles of higher level leadership. The high impact leader has to know when it's time to remove them from the team. How long they wait depends on the level of the leader doing the removing. A lower level leader will put up with it and deal with it hoping they will "turn the corner" and "see the light."

A higher impact leader has more intuition and knows a low level leader that doesn't want to get on board doesn't need to be on board.

When it comes to leading others and intuition, a low level leader's first thought is, "If they report to me, I can make them do it." You'll often hear them tell their boss, "If you want me to make it happen, those people need to start reporting to me.

I need the authority to make things happen." When you hear that statement or one like it, you're witnessing a low level leader seeking power and influence through their position. They know that's all they have. Without the power of position over others, low level leaders have no influence. People simply will not follow them because they don't have to. In this case, timing is irrelevant.

"You are a leader if and only if people follow your leadership when they have the freedom not to."
~ Jim Collins

Timing is not something a low level leader will "waste" their time worrying about. They simply walk in to the meeting with their team or into your office and tell the team or you what to do and when it needs to be done and expect it to happen. It's usually that straightforward. The only time they are worried about is the time it takes you to do what you've been told to do. They are excellent at telling but terrible at selling. Unfortunately, society and organizations around the world are filled with these types of low level leaders.

This book wasn't written for low level leaders. They don't read leadership books. They don't value the principles I'm sharing on these pages. I wrote this book for leaders that want to make a high impact. Leaders that value other people.

High impact leaders must also get others to do certain things in a certain amount of time. But, they do it differently. Leadership is about making things happen. Using influence, high impact leaders get others to buy-in to them and the vision first, which allows them to accomplish the mission together. These high impact leaders know timing gives them leverage.

"A leader is one who sees more than others see, who sees farther than others see, and who sees before others do." ~ Leroy Eims

3 Ways Vision and Timing Leverage Influence

1. **How much leaders "see":** High impact leaders see more than others see. When you see more than others see, you are able to better understand how all of the pieces fit together. You have the advantage of seeing more pieces of the puzzle so to speak. You see more options and have more options. Because you know more about the big picture, you're able to leverage timing by acting on things others can't see. This can be a tremendous advantage and allow you to leverage the talents of your team.

2. **How far leaders "see":** High impact leaders see farther than others see. When you can see farther than others see, you are able to plan for what lies ahead. You have a better idea of when (timing) and where to position key players of your team. You are able to prioritize not only for the short term, but also for the long term. You will have much more leverage over your competition when you can see farther than they can see. You can also work to remove roadblocks for your team before they get to them.

3. **How soon leaders "see":** High impact leaders see before others see. When you see things before others see them, you have leverage because you can start planning sooner. You have the ability to listen to your intuition longer. You have the ability to synergize with others in advance by asking questions and getting feedback. All of this gives a leader the advantage and the ability to leverage influence through timing. In simple terms, you have a head start.

Combine these three areas of advantage high impact leaders have, and you can easily imagine the increased leverage on their influence in all areas. However, timing is still the key that ultimately determines the real advantage.

To further develop your timing skills, start by asking more questions. Become curious about being curious.

Use a beginner's mindset. What does it look like to have a beginner's mindset when it comes to curiosity? It looks very much like the little girl who kept asking her mother question after question. Finally the mother cried, "For heaven's sake, stop asking so many questions. Curiosity killed the cat."

After two minutes of thinking, the little girl asked, "So what did the cat want to know?"[1]

When it comes to learning about timing, the real value comes when you evaluate the outcome. Be sure to reflect on the influence generated by the questions and consider what would have been different had you asked the question sooner or later. How would the influence have been different?

5 Ways to Leverage Timing

"The important thing is not to stop questioning."
~ Albert Einstein

1. **Motivate others to act:** Timing can motivate others to do the right thing at the right time. Asking the right question in advance will get the team to consider it. Asking the right question at the right moment will get the team do it.

2. **Help others to learn:** Timing can help others learn the right thing at the right time. Asking the right question in advance will raise the team's awareness. Asking the right question at the right moment will help the team internalize the lesson.

3. **Inspire others to believe:** Timing can cause others to believe the right thing at the right time. Asking the right question in advance will help the team see it. Asking the right question at the right moment will help the team feel it.

4. **Challenge others to think:** Timing can provoke others to think the right thing at the right time. Asking the right

question in advance will help the team think about options. Asking the right question at the right moment can help the team think about consequences.

5. **Cause others to wait:** Timing can insure others wait for the right thing at the right time. Asking the right question in advance will get the team to slow down. Asking the right question at the right moment will get the team to pause.

> *"My greatest strength as a consultant is to be ignorant and ask a few questions." ~ Peter Drucker*

If you want to increase your influence through timing, you must develop your leadership intuition. The degree to which you learn, apply, and live leadership principles will determine how much intuition you develop and how deeply you understand the impact timing has on your ability to influence others.

High impact leaders always consider the consequences of what they do and when they do it. Leaders evaluate everything with a leadership bias. High impact leaders understand what we've all heard many times before, "Timing is everything!"

> *"Intuition is what we know for sure without knowing for certain" ~ Weston H. Agor*

5

THE VALUE OF RESPECT

To be respected, we must be respectful.

"Go see, ask why, and show respect."
~ Jim Womack

When Jim Womack spoke those words, he was speaking in the context of creating an environment to support continuous improvement (Lean Manufacturing). If you've ever been responsible for leading a support group such as lean, safety, or quality across an organization where everyone is expected to participate, but most do not report to you directly, you will fully understand that without influence, you can't make very much happen.

You must grow and develop yourself into a leader people will naturally want to follow. If you haven't earned respect, be prepared for a lot of frustration.

Even if you have a position of authority over an entire facility or a group of people within a facility, you will lead more effectively with influence than you will with position. If you can set aside your position or formal authority and lead with moral authority, you will have leverage those without a position can't tap into because they don't have a position to set aside. When those reporting to you know you can rule with an iron fist but choose not to, you will gain additional influence and respect. When those reporting to you feel threatened by your power and position, you will lose influence and respect.

"When you compromise who you are, you compromise who you attract." ~ Tony Curl

Low level leaders, with or without a position, demand respect but never get it. High impact leaders, with or without a position, earn respect and have no need to demand it.

Don't be like the low level, positional "boss" in the following short story.

One day a man goes to a pet shop to buy a parrot. The assistant takes the man to the parrot section and asks the man to choose one. The man asks, "How much is the yellow one?"

The assistant says, "$2,000." The man is shocked and asks the assistant why it's so expensive.

The assistant explains, "This parrot is very, very special. He knows typewriting and can type really fast."

"What about the green one?" the man asks.

The assistant says, "He costs $5,000 because he knows typewriting, can answer incoming phone calls, and take notes."

"What about the red one?" the man asks.

The assistant says, "That one is $10,000."

The man says, "What does HE do?"

The assistant says, "I don't know, but the other two call him boss."[1]

It may be hard for some to believe, but this is the way it is with many leaders in the real world too. Unfortunately, many leaders do not interact with their teams very much, if at all. They're afraid they may somehow become responsible if they get too close. In these cases, the team doesn't know what the "boss" does, and the "boss" doesn't know what the team is doing. High impact leaders get to know their team and build strong relationships with them.

When you follow someone only because of their position, you're only doing it because you have to. When you follow someone because you respect them, you're following them because you want to.

When people follow you because they have to, your influence with them is weak. When people follow you because they want to, your influence with them is strong.

Respecting a position and respecting a person are not the same thing.

- When I respect your position, I usually do what's expected. When I respect you, I often do more than is expected.
- When I respect your position, I usually show up on time. When I respect you, I often show up ahead of time.
- When I respect your position, I usually follow the process. When I respect you, I often improve the process.
- When I respect your position, I usually tell you there is a problem.
  When I respect you, I often tell you what I did to solve the problem.

"When people respect you as a person, they admire you. When they respect you as a friend, they love you. When they respect you as a leader, they follow you."
~ John C. Maxwell

As Jim Womack says, "Go see, ask why, and show respect." Let's consider how these three actions can and will increase your influence and moral authority.

All three components Jim mentioned are associated with earning respect. True leadership (influence) is very fluid and dynamic. As situations and circumstances change, the leader must remain flexible and adapt to the changes. Principles never change, but practices often do. The principle here is the leader must maintain flexibility and avoid rigidity. When there is a problem, a challenge, or an opportunity, we should "Go see, ask why, and show respect."

Go See

"One never does wrong by doing right."
~ Norman Vincent Peale

No matter your position, if you want to know what's going on, quit asking. Go get in the middle of it. I guarantee you will find out because that's where the answer is. When you ask others, there's often much you're not being told. You may not be told on purpose, or you may not be told because the messenger doesn't know because they didn't *go see* for themselves. You can't blame them for following the leader. What do I mean? If you want them to *go see*, then you must *go see*. When you do, take them with you.

When I start working with an organization where no one normally *goes to see*, the first thing I do is determine the highest level person I can get to *go see* with me. If I can get the top leader to *go see* with me, all of those reporting to him or her will automatically start *going to see*. Why? Because they don't want the leader to learn something they don't know. Amazing how this principle works. If you want your team to start *going to see*, all you have to do is start *going to see* yourself.

If it's truly important for you to know the truth, don't go ask; *go see*. Model the behavior for others. Every layer between you and the people that know what you want to know serves as a filter. Every time the information passes through someone, it gets diluted.

Personally, I never want to get the answer to a question from someone that doesn't know the answer. To me, that doesn't even make sense. I want to talk to the person that knows the answer, not the person that thinks they know the answer.

However, what I've observed more often than not, is a leader will often ask someone reporting to them what's going on. That person may think they know based on past experience and give an answer. Or, they may ask someone reporting to them for the answer. That person may or may not know but are usually happy to give their best guess as a fact (the answer). Too many times, the "answer" is given without anyone ever *going to see*. They may think they know the answer, and they may or may not be right. But, if I'm going to make a decision about something, I want to know I know the answer, not think I know the answer.

Going to see is one of the first things I do when I support a company relative to process improvement. Why? I want to truly know what's happening. I don't want to know what everyone thinks is happening. Very seldom does what I'm told match what I *see*. There is always a gap between knowing and *seeing*.

Most often, I'm challenged with getting the leaders out of the office, off of the computer, and in front of the issue. Typically, they think they know, or they think those informing them know. Too often though, nobody knows except those at the source doing the real work, and they're seldom being asked.

It amazes me how often I can be in a company for only a few days and know more about the real issues holding them back than those that have been working there for years. Frequently, I find they have become complacent. They simply think they already know all the answers. That's a costly mistake.

Who will earn more respect? Someone that thinks they know what is going on or someone that truly knows what's going on?

The key is understanding when you *go see* you can dig deeper and *ask why*.

Ask Why

"Start strong, stay strong, and finish strong by always remembering why you're doing it in the first place."
~ Ralph Marston

Asking why empowers others by transferring leadership (influence) to the person answering the question. They can be the "boss" for a moment. They have been liberated and now have a voice. It changes everything. You are also now sharing the responsibility for solving the issue or making an improvement. They now have the power to influence you and anyone else listening.

Asking why demonstrates your value for the other person's knowledge, thoughts, and opinions. *Asking why* allows you to earn respect. Telling someone how, when you really don't know, and they know you don't know, will definitely cause you to lose respect. Too often, low level leaders, that don't *go see*, often want to tell others how to improve or solve the problem which often leads to other problems.

Often in my leadership or lean training classes, I'll ask those in the audience what it means when someone asks "why" you're doing something. The most frequent answer is, "they think I'm doing it wrong." Actually, that is often the reason low level leaders *ask why*. But, in an environment where we are trying to improve the processes or solve problems by getting to the root cause of an issue, we simply *ask why* because we really want to know *why*.

To illustrate in a training session, I ask them what it means when a five year old *asks why* they are doing something. They instantly answer, "Because they want to learn." I tell them that's the same reason a high impact leader *asks why*. They want to learn too, not blame. I make sure they know I'm going to be *asking why* simply because I want to learn. I want to know *why*.

When you demonstrate humility and have a desire to learn, you earn respect. You are not weak. You are strong.

Insecure leaders don't *ask why*. They tell how. Insecure leaders don't earn respect. Only secure leaders earn respect from others.

When you *ask why*, be sure to listen for the answer. When you do, that shows respect.

Show Respect

"You can judge a man's character by the way he treats those who can't help him or hurt him." ~ *Mack Story*

If you want to earn respect, *show respect*. There are many ways to *show respect*. We've just discussed two: *go see* and *ask why*.

When you *go see*, you are showing respect for those doing the real work by showing up. They are proud of what they do. If you *go see*, that is one of the things you will see. Most people are naturally good and want to do good work. When they feel respected, they become more respectful. When they do, they want to do better work.

When you *ask why*, you are *showing respect* for them as a person. When you *ask why*, the other person instantly feels respected. If you listen, they will continue to feel respected. Not only will you earn respect from those you are *asking why*, but you will also earn respect from those watching and listening.

When people respect you, they will talk good about you. As a result, you will also earn respect from those that will learn about your concern for the opinions of those closest to the process. When they don't respect you, they don't talk good about you. They just talk about you.

People who *go see*, *ask why*, and *show respect* are demonstrating strong character. The stronger your character, the greater your influence. If you want to lead high level leaders, you must live your life at a high level. Not just when you're at work, but when you're not at work. As I've mentioned, your influence in the world is based on who you are 24 hours a day, 7 days a week, 365 days a year.

Who we are sometime is who we are all the time.

What I mean is if we pretend to be one way at work or around certain people or in certain places but are different other times when we are with our friends or when we think no one is looking, that's who we truly are. We're the same person whether we're behind the curtain or in front of it. What people may see is different, but who we are is the same. Again, who we are sometime is who we are all of the time when it comes to our character.

We are not who we pretend to be. We are who we are when we're not pretending. Although we may try to hide who we truly are from others, that doesn't change the fact of who we really are on the inside. It's all about congruency of character. If you can't be the same person all the time, you've got character work to do.

If you want to be respected, be respectable. You cannot hide from who you are. Neither can you hide who you are from others for very long. Everywhere you go, there you are.

"When you treat people like idiots, they will often meet your expectations." ~ Linda Kaplan Thaler

6

THE VALUE OF EMPOWERMENT

Leaders gain influence by giving it to others.

"Leadership is not reserved for leaders."
~ Marcus Buckingham

The key to living the *Value of Empowerment* is understanding the difference between empowerment and disengagement.

High impact leaders leverage empowerment to unleash their team's potential.

Lower level leaders do not empower. Instead, they practice disengagement in the name of empowerment. As a result, they create distrust among the team. They talk empowerment, but they walk disengagement. They are not congruent.

Disengagement is when a leader pretends to empower you but only allows you to make decisions he/she approves. They will stay out of the way until they need to do a course correction in the direction you're heading. Once they've made the adjustment, they disappear again.

An empowering leader does not disappear. They are always alongside you to support and help you accomplish the mission. They may not always be there physically and shouldn't always be there physically, but they are there when you need them to be there. They support the team instead of directing the team. They are one voice, but not the only voice.

Secure leaders understand when they give power to others they do not lose power themselves. They focus on releasing their team. Secure leaders lead with an abundance mindset and understand there is plenty of everything for everyone. They give credit, power, recognition, and control to the team.

When they give power to others, insecure leaders incorrectly believe they somehow have less power. Therefore, they focus on controlling the team. Insecure leaders lead with a scarcity mindset and falsely believe everything is limited. They feel the need to take credit, hold on to power, avoid recognition, and maintain control.

"I was not interested in flattery or fluff. Rigidity gets in the way of creativity. Instead of salutes, I wanted results." ~ Captain D. Michael Abrashoff

10 Ways Secure Leaders Differ From Insecure Leaders

1. Delegation

Secure leaders delegate the desired results, not methods. When we delegate results, we are transferring responsibility for methods to those doing the work. When those doing the work determine the method, they take ownership in achieving the results. Since they're responsible for methods and ultimately results, they are flexible and can change methods to effectively and efficiently achieve the desired results.

Insecure leaders delegate methods in order to achieve the desired results. By doing so, they retain full responsibility for the results. When those doing the work are told what to do, they avoid ownership of the results. They are rigid and simply do as they're told. As a result, whatever happens, happens.

2. Decision Making

Secure leaders empower others by giving them the power to make decisions. The team members know they are responsible, but they also know the leader is there to support them. The leader comes alongside when needed, but doesn't take over. The secure leader's role is to facilitate decision making. Even when the team asks for help, the secure leader doesn't give them answers, he leads by asking them questions.

Insecure leaders disengage in the name of empowerment by giving others the "false impression" they have the ability to make decisions. The insecure leader is always hovering over and smothering "snoopervising" to ensure the right decisions are made. If they think it's right, they say nothing. If they think it's wrong, they re-engage and make the decision. Insecure leaders think their role is to make decisions. When the team asks for help, the insecure leader jumps in with the answers.

3. Trust

Secure leaders know the power of empowerment comes when those on the team truly feel trusted. When they feel trust, they know they are ultimately responsible. They know the leader is counting on them to accomplish the mission. They know unless they ask for help, the leader assumes everything is on track.

Insecure leaders exhibit false trust by disengaging and stepping back while attempting to make those carrying out the mission feel as though they are responsible. They only pretend to trust. But, they are never far away. They are always "keeping an eye" on what's going on. If they see something questionable, they get involved and start making course corrections. Then, disengage again in the name of empowerment.

4. Teamwork

Secure leaders expect the team to synergize. They empower others to determine methods because they know there will be unlimited synergistic solutions to problems as they arise. They clearly define the desired results and get out of the way. They expect the team to work together to develop solutions.

Insecure leaders marginalize their team. They typically provide one unilateral solution. They are so busy making decisions for everyone that they don't have time to listen to anyone. If their first idea doesn't work, they provide another. They limit the team by not allowing them to adjust midstream when they realize there may be a problem. The team feels bound to carry out the leader's order.

5. Thinking

Secure leaders want their team to do all of the thinking. They know that's where and when they will grow the most. They understand all growth happens outside of the comfort zone. They often intentionally challenge their team members to find new solutions to old problems.

Insecure leaders want to do all of the thinking. What's interesting is you will often hear them complaining about their team, "I don't know why they can't ever think for themselves." The reason is because the leader is always thinking for them. Whenever there is a mistake, the insecure leader hurriedly offers a solution. It's like a parent that says, "I don't know why my 17 year old can't think for himself?" It's because the parent has always told them what to do without helping them learn to think by asking them thought provoking questions.

6. Belief

Secure leaders believe in their team. They don't just say it. They demonstrate it. They don't have to say it because their team members feel it. When you believe in others, it releases them to achieve what they may not have thought was possible. They are borrowing belief from you. When their team makes a mistake, the leader believes they learned a valuable lesson during the process. As a result, the team is much more likely to expose problems in order to correct and learn from them.

Insecure leaders believe in themselves and discount their team. They question their team's actions constantly. They shoot down their ideas regularly and frequently. Members of the team often feel anxiety while carrying out the mission. They are always wondering, "Am I doing it right?" They feel constricted by the pressure of doing it the leader's way instead of their own way. When an insecure leader's team makes a mistake, they are punished and ridiculed. In the future, the team is much more likely to hide problems out of fear. Therefore, instead of being addressed, problems are intentionally hidden.

7. Support

Secure leaders come alongside their team. They are not out front pulling. Nor are they in the back pushing. They are in a support role. They understand their job is to remove the obstacles for the team. They are the team's biggest cheerleader. The team loves to have them around.

Insecure leaders are always pulling or pushing their teams. Why? For the insecure leader, it's not about the team. It's about themselves. Their goal is not to grow and support the team during the process. Their goal is to get the results they want when they want them. The team hopes they don't come around.

8. Credit

Secure leaders love to give credit to others. They don't need it. They look for opportunities to give recognition to the team. When things go right, they look through the window and give credit to the team. When things go wrong, they look in the mirror and take the blame. They believe they somehow let the team down. They feel there was something they could have and should have done to help.

Insecure leaders seek the credit. They feed on it. They look for things to go right, so they can take credit from the team. When things go right, they look in the mirror and take the credit. When things go wrong, they look through the window and blame the team. They avoid any responsibility. Remember, the leader is either making it happen, allowing it to happen, or preventing it from happening. If not, someone else is leading.

9. Control

Secure leaders exhibit passion. They motivate and inspire others to take action. They are most excited when they have inspired others to make things happen through motivation. They are energized when they release others to freely find their way. They trust the team to carry out the mission.

Insecure leaders thrive on control. They give orders to move others to action. They're most excited when they are in control making things happen through the manipulation of others. They are most energized when they get their way. They must know what is going on.

10. Process

Secure leaders have grown accustomed to challenging the process. Therefore, they encourage others to challenge the process. The most secure leaders want the processes they put in place to be challenged by their team. The secure leader's motto is, "Say no to the status quo." Those challenging the process are the most highly valued.

Insecure leaders do not want to rock the boat. They also don't want their team to rock the boat. They value the status quo and will do everything in their power to maintain it. Processes they put in place are the "sacred cows" or are not discussable. They think, "If it's not broke, don't fix it."

"Leaders can't stand the status quo. They don't lay in bed and dream of how things are. They dream of how things could be." ~ Andy Stanley

If you want to be a high impact leader, you must develop yourself to the level where you can truly leverage the power that comes from empowering your team. If you can't empower the team, it's not their fault. It's your fault. If you think it's not, you have more character work to do. High impact leaders are always responsible to their team. However, they are not always responsible for their team. If the team is truly empowered, they are responsible for themselves.

It should never be about the leader, but it should always be about the team. High impact leaders fully understand this. President Abraham Lincoln made this point very clearly in story I read a year or so ago.

The President would often sit in the telegraph office receiving the very latest reports from the battlefields. One night a telegraph message came in detailing yet another Union army calamity. Confederate cavalry had surprised a Union camp near Manassas, Virginia, and captured a brigadier general and a hundred horses. With the telegraph operator watching,

Lincoln slumped in his chair as he read of this latest setback. Moaning slightly he said, "Sure hate to lose those hundred horses."

The operator felt obliged to ask, "Mr. President, what about the brigadier general?"

Lincoln replied, "I can make a brigadier general in five minutes, but it is not easy to replace one hundred horses."

President Lincoln surely valued the brigadier general, but he also knew without the hundred horses, another brigadier general wasn't going to do him very much good.

General Colin Powell actually shared this story about Lincoln in his book, *It Worked for Me: In Life and Leadership*. General Powell had this to say in reference to the story about Lincoln, "My job as leader was to take care of the horses, get the most out of them, and make sure they were all pulling in the direction I wanted to go. And, by the way, make sure there were folks behind me ready to be promoted to brigadier general and take over after I left."

It's not about the leader. It's about the team. Leaders don't do the work. They get the work done. A high impact leader never forgets that simple fact.

To make this point clear during his welcoming speech for then Brigadier General Powell and 58 of his new fellow brigadier generals, Army Chief of Staff General Bernie Rogers put it this way, "If I put you all in a plane, and it crashed with no survivors. The next 59 names on that list will be just as good as you. No problem."

General Rogers was making it clear to the brigadier generals that they had not arrived. He wanted them to perfectly understand they were not special, and it was important that they didn't think they were.

It's not about the leader. It's about the team. A leader has to value the horses and what they allow him to accomplish. Without the horses to literally move the mission forward, there will be no mission.

7

THE VALUE OF DELEGATION

We should lead with questions instead of directions.

"Delegation 101: Delegating 'what to do,' makes you responsible. Delegating 'what to accomplish,' allows others to become responsible."
~ Mack Story

It's much easier to lead others using questions instead of directions.

Many leaders do not understand true delegation is a tool that can be used to grow their team and strengthen their relationships. During my many years of Lean Manufacturing consulting, I led many cross-functional teams with varying process improvement goals. I would typically have one week to get results with a group of strangers. How hard could that be right?

Over the years, I learned to be very effective at delegating. Not the old "do this and do that" kind of delegation most people think of when they hear the word delegation. That isn't leadership of people, but rather management of people. It's low level delegation and doesn't promote growth, responsibility, or ownership.

High impact delegation empowers individuals and teams to thrive and grow. I first heard Dr. Stephen R. Covey speak on *The 5 Levels of Stewardship Delegation* many years ago. As I applied and taught them, I also enhanced my understanding of them which has allowed me to add to and enhance how I define and teach them. I call my version *The 5 Levels of High Impact Delegation.*

You must understand these principles apply not only personally, with our children, family, or friends, but also professionally with those we work with whether they report directly to us or not. High impact delegation is about growth and development not authority.

> *"Never delegate methods, only results."*
> *~ Dr. Stephen R. Covey*

The 5 Levels of High Impact Delegation

1. Wait for Directions – No growth. No respect. No responsibility. A low level leader simply tells the person or team what to do. The leader may not even be aware they have finished the last task. Either way, when they're finished, they *wait for directions*.

They keep *waiting* until they are told what to do next. This is absolutely the lowest level of delegation and, unfortunately, the most common. It's quick and efficient. It's also very effective, short term. Low level leaders love it. It's also very ineffective and an absolute waste of time, long term. High impact leaders avoid it.

Many people delegate at this level continuously with their associates at work and their children at home while wondering why they can't get them to think for themselves. How will they ever learn to think for themselves when they never have to? At this level, the leader does all of the thinking and is responsible for the effectiveness and the outcome.

A low level leader values control and leads from a position of authority. A high impact leader values release and sets aside their position (if they have one) and leads with influence.

2. Ask What's Next – No growth. No respect. Only a very small amount of responsibility. Once they have completed the delegated task, the low level leader instructs the person or team to *ask what's next*.

What small responsibility do they have? When they have finished, they must find the leader and simply *ask what's next*.

That's it! No growth and development at this level either. The leader will see a slight increase in productivity because he/she is able to keep the person or team busy without as much *waiting*.

However, the leader still does all of the thinking and is responsible for determining what they should and will do next. At least, the leader knows when they've completed their last assigned task. Then, another task can be assigned.

Only low level leaders (managers that like to direct people) delegate at Levels 1 and 2. High impact leaders (leaders that like to develop people) know the value of delegating and delegate at Level 3 or above intentionally.

"Before you attempt to set things right, make sure you see things right." ~ Blaine Lee

3. Recommend a Course of Action – Growth happens. Respect is mutual. Responsibility is transferred. Everything changes at this level. Thinking is now a shared responsibility. The leader values the person or team's experience, their opinions, and their decision making ability.

The responsibility for determining and suggesting the next task has been transferred to the person or team carrying out the task. They are now required to think before approaching the leader with a recommendation.

When they do, the leader can now evaluate their thought process. If the leader disagrees, he/she does not revert back to Level 1 or 2. Instead, the leader facilitates additional thought and decision making by asking thought provoking questions to help the person or team think more deeply while considering the cause and effect of their recommendation. This allows both parties to learn from each other and understand the situation better.

Often, the leader will learn from the team and agree with their recommendation. Other times, the leader will not agree and ask more questions until mutual agreement is reached on a course of action. However, the responsibility always remains with the person or team being delegated to.

The leader is now in a support role growing and developing the person or team. As the leader learns to trust their thinking and decision making, he is able to move them to higher levels of delegation. If he doesn't yet trust them, he can continue asking questions to help shape and refine their thought process and understanding of the bigger picture.

"If we're starting with the wrong questions, if we don't understand the cause, then even the right answers will always steer us wrong." ~ Simon Sinek

A high impact leader will also never take back responsibility for very important or critical project work because this will create an atmosphere of distrust resulting in low morale. If the task is critical or very important, the leader may move back to Level 3 from either Level 4 or 5 because they need to be informed or want to assist in the thought process by asking questions. Under no circumstance will a high impact leader take ownership of and complete the task. This would be very disrespectful and reduce the leader's influence. Often, low level leaders will complete highly important or highly visible tasks because they want the credit for themselves.

4. Do It and Report Immediately – Additional, but limited, responsibility is transferred. The leader has more trust and confidence in the person or team and allows them to accept the responsibility of choosing and then completing the next task without support.

At this level, the person or team has limited authority to make their decision and take action. Then, they notify the leader of what has been done before taking the next additional action.

Because the action is complete before the leader is informed, the person or team now feels a greater responsibility because their thoughts are determining the outcome (on a small scale). They are starting to fully own the process one small step at a time.

The leader can choose to be flexible and give boundaries or limits. It doesn't have to literally be every single step. It could easily be groups of steps at natural intervals of completion relative to a single process or project.

5. Own It and Report Routinely – Full responsibility has been transferred. At this level, the person or team reports to the leader at predetermined intervals (end of project(s), days, weeks, or even months, or only when the person or team feels it is necessary). The leader trusts the person or team completely and is confident in their ability to make the right decisions.

"Rarely is delegation failure the subordinate's fault. Maybe you picked the wrong person for the job, didn't train, develop or motivate sufficiently." ~ Ken Allen

Don't give up on delegation even if you have struggled with it in the past. I've found most people don't delegate because they feel they don't have enough time. I've also found most people don't have time because they don't delegate. When it comes to delegation, short term thinking (I don't have time.) will prevent you from making the time which will save you time (long term).

For instance, if it takes you an hour per week to do a task (52 hours per year). And, let's say it would take you 10 hours over 10 weeks to train someone else to do the task. If you think you're too busy and don't have the 10 hours it will take to train someone, you will spend 52 hours per year doing this task yourself.

However, if you make the time to train and then delegate the task to someone, you will save 32 hours the first year alone. (52 hours required to do it - 10 hours doing the task yourself - 10 hours training someone else to do it = 32 hours saved in the first year!) You don't have time not to delegate!

Now, this person can help you train and develop others too. Not only do you save this time, but you work on delegating more tasks to others and continue to free up your time. Don't just tell them what to do. That's Level 1 delegation. Help them learn how to think at a higher level.

Key Points

When delegating, it's always best to start at Level 3. This allows the leader to learn how the person, team, or child thinks. Level 3 allows the leader to engage them in the thought process. As they build trust over time, the leader can then move them up to the higher levels of delegation. As the leader moves others into the higher levels of delegation, the leader will gain more discretionary time to accomplish other tasks.

Depending on the task, the leader may select to move someone from Level 5 back to Level 4 or 3. They should only do this in order to either participate in the thought process or to be informed of the progress related to a special or new project. Moving someone to a lower level of delegation is always intentional and usually temporary.

With trust, we always know. Without trust, we never know.

With trust, things happen fast. Without trust, things happen slowly, if at all.

With trust, everything is possible. Without trust, everything is questioned.

With trust, relationships grow. Without trust, relationships wither.

"The beauty of trust is that it erases worry and frees you to get on with other matters. Trust means confidence." ~ Stephen M. R. Covey

8

THE VALUE OF MULTIPLICATION

None of us is as influential as all of us.

"To add growth, lead followers. To multiply, lead leaders." ~ John C. Maxwell

Make no mistake, every one of us is a leader, but we lead at different levels. Leadership is influence, and everyone has it. However, those typically leading have more influence than those typically following.

Ultimately, we are all leaders, and we are all followers. The best leaders know when it's best to lead and when it's best to follow. They know and understand leadership is very dynamic.

There is nothing wrong with being a follower. If you are a follower, then be the best follower you can be. We must be good followers before we can choose to become great leaders. If you're content with following, you should spend a little time reflecting and asking yourself, "What am I leaving on the table?" More importantly, "Why am I choosing not to develop my potential?"

You are fully capable of climbing the leadership ladder and increasing your influence which will increase your options. If you're not slowly, steadily, methodically, and intentionally working to increase your influence, why not? It's the only thing that will move you forward. Everything rises and falls on influence.

This chapter is not about those typically following, but I need to clarify my perspective on the terms follower and leader in order to help you effectively understand my frame of reference when using these terms.

By definition, a follower is also a leader because they influence others. However, the term *follower* represents a lower level leader on the leadership scale from 1-10. The term *leader* represents a higher level leader on the leadership scale from 1-10.

The higher up the scale the leader is, the higher up the scale his/her followers will be. No matter their level, leaders attract a "tribe" or group that volunteers to follow because of who the leader is (character), what the leader knows (competency), and where the leader is going (vision).

Within the subgroup of leader referred to as *followers*, there is also a range. There are low level followers and high impact followers. A low level follower may follow the leader somewhat blindly and has very little influence left or right with their peers or above with their leader or leaders of others. These followers are doing all they can do to follow effectively. A high impact follower has influence left and right with their peers and also above with their leader and leaders of others.

Typically, a low level follower does less than is expected alone, and a high impact follower does more than is expected with others.

"Don't reorganize around a weak follower. Retrain, move, or fire them. You're doing that person a favor in the long term. And, you are doing your team a favor immediately." ~ General Colin Powell

5 Traits of High Impact Followers

1. **They add value to the leader.** They make the leader better by looking for ways to help the leader. They do this by doing more than is expected, doing things before they are expected, and doing things better than expected. They also provide valuable unsolicited insight and feedback to the leader.

2. **They value the leader.** They support the leader. They understand their leader is also their #1 customer. They respect their leader and demonstrate it through their dedication and quality of work.

3. **They add value to the team.** They make the team better by looking for ways to help others excel. They look for ways to help those that need to be helped. They give credit to the team instead of accepting it for themselves. They develop and nurture sustainable relationships throughout the team.

4. **They value the team.** They appreciate the differences of each team member. They express gratitude freely and openly. They offer support and share ideas abundantly. They don't focus on me, but instead focus on we.

5. **They invest in personal growth.** This is a trait reserved for the most developed high impact followers. They are on their way to becoming high impact leaders. They don't wait for anyone to develop them. They develop themselves on purpose for a purpose. As they do, others begin to follow them.

They will still be capable of following as all great leaders are, but while they are following, others will be following them. When this happens, they have completed the transition from follower to leader. They may not have a formal leadership position yet. But, it's only a matter of time before they will be recognized for their influence and offered one.

"Moral leaders exercise power for good purposes. Essential to this is that they do not hoard power; they give it away. There is no leadership without power. However, a leader will frequently want to distribute rather than to maintain power. Leaders empower their followers." ~ Terry A. Smith

If we want to see growth in our organization, we simply lead followers willing to get things done. However, if we want to see explosive growth, we must learn to lead leaders willing to move beyond getting things done. Leaders that will make things happen!

High impact leaders say no to the status quo while others hate to see it go.

While followers maintain the status quo, high impact leaders are looking for ways to grow. Followers are great for maintaining the gains, but they are often resistant to creating the change. Leaders are not satisfied with only maintaining the gains. They look for opportunities to improve themselves, their team, and their organization. They live by the motto: "Without change, there can be no improvement."

There are also subgroups within the group referred to as *leaders*. There are low level leaders and high impact leaders.

A low level leader attracts lower level followers. This low level leader is doing their best to unleash and lead their followers effectively. On the other hand, a high impact leader attracts not only followers, but also other leaders and is primarily focused on developing those leaders. Typically, a low level leader directly leads their followers, but a high impact leader not only directly leads other leaders, but also indirectly leads their followers.

- Low level leaders are satisfied with accidental growth. High impact leaders are passionate about intentional growth.
- Low level leaders are focused on success. High impact leaders are focused on significance.
- Low level leaders get it done. High impact leaders make things happen!

"Good leaders look at people's strength and make use of it; great leaders look at people's potential and make the best of it." ~ Denis G. McLaughlin

7 Traits of High Impact Leaders

1. **Continuously invest in themselves.** High impact leaders know the most important thing they must never stop doing is developing themselves. They know they can't grow other leaders or their organization beyond their own leadership ability. High impact leaders are relentless in their pursuit of growth and spend countless hours and thousands of dollars on their own personal development. Without this hunger to grow and develop their own leadership ability, they would be just another leader among the masses getting mediocre results.

The side effect of their passion: they have amazing teams that are always achieving amazing results.

2. **Continuously invest in their top leaders.** High impact leaders are not selfish and stingy when it comes to growing their leaders. They live with an abundance mentality. When they identify a high potential leader, they put them on an accelerated leadership development program. They expect their top leaders to be fully engaged at all times with leadership development. As a result, they make the funds available, allow them time for development, and encourage them to attend leadership training seminars and leadership certification programs.

High impact leaders know this: the return on developing their leaders, although hard to measure, is greater than the cost.

3. **Create and maintain an internal leadership program.** High impact leaders take leadership in their organizations to a very high level. They create an internal, ongoing leadership program for their entire team from top to bottom. They train the trainers. They not only have outside leadership professionals come in to help develop their top leaders and themselves, but they and their top leaders actively engage in training their lower level leaders

and followers. High impact leaders know the best way to learn leadership is to teach leadership because it makes them accountable for modeling what they teach.

4. Focus on the strengths of their leaders. High impact leaders quickly identify the strengths of their leaders. They want to leverage the strengths and ignore the weaknesses. They know when a leader is allowed to work in their strength zone, they are unstoppable. They know nothing energizes a leader like results. When leaders are allowed and encouraged to work in their strength zone, they exhibit high energy and experience a deep passion, while simultaneously motivating and inspiring others around them to action. High impact leaders make sure their leaders are intentionally positioned within the organization to take advantage of their strengths. They don't wait for it to happen by accident. High impact leaders make it happen intentionally.

5. Do not treat leaders the same. High impact leaders do not hesitate to reward leaders doing the right things. Not only are they rewarded, but they are publicly acknowledged for their contribution. If you want to see your top leaders walk out the door, treat them like a mediocre leader. In an explosive growth atmosphere, high impact leaders are not treated the same. They learn more, so they earn more. They lead by example, so they are made to be the example. High impact leaders are quick to shine the light on the behavior they want to see in other leaders. They spend more time with them, ask them more questions, and give them high profile special assignments.

They send the message: "If there's any doubt, this is what I'm looking for in a leader."

6. Make time for their leaders. High impact leaders invest time with their leaders. They tend to apply the 80/20 rule. They spend 80% of their time with the top 20% of their leaders. The top 20% are typically responsible for 80% of the results in the organization. Low level leaders do just the opposite. They spend 80% of their time with the bottom 20% of their leaders trying to get them on board. What a waste of time! They are not on board because they don't want to be on board. Focus on those wanting to make things happen, and they will make things happen.

Schedule meetings with your top leaders, go to lunch with your top leaders, or schedule an off-site leadership retreat for the top 20%. That's really a win-win because everyone gets to grow together on purpose for a purpose. These top 20% leaders will lead and develop the other 80% for you.

7. **Give their leaders more responsibility.** High impact leaders feed the need. They know their leaders want to do more, be more, and have more. They take their leaders outside of their comfort zone and place them in the growth zone. They continually challenge their leaders to grow by giving them ever increasing responsibilities that stretch them beyond their current level of awareness. High impact leaders know when a leader isn't being stretched, they aren't being challenged to reach their full potential. They're leaving a lot on the table.

Stretching does not come naturally to everyone. There's a story about a country boy called Bubba who was once offered a full-time job by a landowner who was having problems with beavers building dams on his property. The landowner hired Bubba to rid the creek of all the beaver and even provided a rifle for him to use.

Bubba was excited because it had been a while since he had a regular payday. Not long after he started, a friend stopped by to see Bubba and found him sitting on a grassy bank, kicked back with the gun across his lap. "Hey Bubba, what's up?" he asked.

"Working," said Bubba half asleep.

"Working on what?"

"Getting rid of the beaver in this creek."

His friend looked over at the creek, and just about that time a beaver popped up from beneath the water. "There's one!" the friend exclaimed. "Shoot it Bubba!"

Bubba didn't even wiggle. Meanwhile the beaver dove back under. "Why didn't' you shoot it Bubba?"

"Are you crazy?" replied Bubba. "Do you think I want to lose my job?"

As this simple story reveals, not everyone is looking to stretch themselves. Many are happy to simply coast along and maintain the status quo. But, for a high impact leader, stretching themselves and others is a part of their mission.

"Everyone chooses one of two roads in life- the old and the young, the rich and the poor, men and women alike. One is the broad, well-traveled road to mediocrity, the other the road to greatness and meaning." ~ Dr. Stephen R. Covey

Many leaders want the benefits of multiplication but are unwilling to pay the price to attain it. Therefore, they remain at the helm of a mediocre team or continue leading a mediocre organization. It's not the people's fault. It's the leader's fault.

Before you can lead others to explosive growth, you must experience explosive growth. If you haven't achieved explosive growth in your personal life relative to character growth, start there. If you have, the next step is to define and refine a competency that will allow you to grow professionally. As you achieve results personally and professionally, you must continue to invest in developing yourself in order to one day be in a position to invest in and develop others.

"In times of change, learners inherit the earth, while the learned find themselves beautifully equipped to deal with a world that no longer exists." ~ Eric Hoffer

9

THE VALUE OF RESULTS

Leaders like to make things happen.

"Most people fail in the getting started."
~ Maureen Falcone

Leaders make things happen. Not just for themselves, but also for their teams. It's who they are. They don't think, "Can we?" or "Will we?" High impact leaders think, "How can we?" and "When will we?" They have a completely different mindset than lower level leaders.

I've led hundreds of cross-functional teams with great success on some very challenging process improvement projects. As a Lean Manufacturing consultant, I didn't have authority over anyone in the facility or on the team. I was an outsider. No one had to follow me.

I had to lead with influence as high impact leaders do. I'm going to share 10 tips that will help you help your team get results. These 10 tips are essential if you want to elevate the success of any team. Timing is also critical as we discussed previously. Knowing when to do what you do will always be an important consideration.

The most important underlying principle that will allow you to effectively benefit from these 10 tips is to understand you must not only do what is necessary, but you must also do it only when (*Value of Timing*) it is necessary and if it is necessary.

"Start doing what is necessary; then, do what is possible; and suddenly you are doing the impossible." ~ St. Francis of Assisi

As a high impact leader, your job is to make sure you and your team don't settle for doing only what's necessary. You must help them discover what is truly possible. This reminds me of a funny story about settling.

A man went to a fortune-teller to hear what she had to say about his future results. She looked into a crystal ball and said, "You will be poor and unhappy until you are forty-five years old."

"Then what will happen?" asked the man hopefully.

"Then you'll get used to it."[1]

High impact leaders don't "get used to it." They don't settle for the status quo. They make things happen, and then, they make some more things happen.

Set the bar higher for your team than they set it for themselves. Stretch them. Believe in them. Support them. And ultimately, help them win.

10 Proven Tips to Help Your Team Win

1. Lead the team when necessary.

It's the leader's responsibility to chart the course. If you are not seeing movement or the movement is in the wrong direction, you must either create movement or make a course correction. I don't mean you take over and start barking orders. That's not leading (influencing). That's managing (directing).

Remember, we lead people, and we manage stuff (things and processes). Ask the right questions until they see what you see or until you see what they see. Once everyone is aligned and back on track, get out of the way.

"Progress is always preceded by change. Change is always preceded by challenge. Where there is no challenge there is no change. It's the job of the leader to challenge the process." ~ Andy Stanley

2. Get out of the team's way when necessary.

If the team is on track moving in the right direction, they don't need you out front. You'll only be a distraction. Distractions slow a team down. If they've got it, let them have it. Get out of the way and lead.

If you must to do something, consider the following tips. Don't put yourself out front unless it's necessary. You have more important things to do than lead the train down the track.

"Superior leadership is often a matter of superb instinct." ~ General Colin Powell

3. Follow the team when necessary.

If you want to boost a team's confidence, follow them. In other words, you let them lead you. You may have heard the old saying, "The best leaders also make the best followers." This is the application of that principle. When the team hears and sees you agreeing with their suggestions, you are reinforcing their decision-making abilities.

They need to feel you believe they are on the right track. Nothing says this more clearly than when the leader is following the team.

"A good leader inspires people to have confidence in the leader; a great leader inspires people to have confidence in themselves." ~ Eleanor Roosevelt

4. Clear the team's path when necessary.

The team will encounter obstacles. Some they can clear without much effort. Let them do it. But, if they get hung up, get out front and help them remove the obstacles.

When leading teams in organizations as a consultant, this is one of the things I request from top leaders. I let them know up front, "I'm counting on you to remove any obstacles we encounter that are too difficult or time consuming for us to spend time and energy on." Many times for a top level leader to remove an obstacle for us, all we need is a signature or an approval to move forward.

"A true friend doesn't just warn you about a stone in your path that may cause you to fall, they do their best to keep you from falling. If that is not possible, they are there to help you back up." ~ Denis G. McLaughlin

5. Help the team when necessary.

When your team needs help, help them. Don't let them learn the hard way if you know the easy way. That doesn't build trust. It creates distrust. Helping is a very effective way to strengthen relationships by building trust.

I remember a 5S (standardization and organization) event I was leading once in a facility. At the time, I was the Lean (Process Improvement) Manager there. We were conducting a week-long event in an area that required a lot of painting. Four days into the five day event, it was obvious there wouldn't be enough time for the team to complete the project. I decided to help.

After they left for the day, around 5pm, I started painting and didn't quit until the next morning when they came back in at 7am. I helped them for 14 hours overnight without being asked. The result: they finished the event on time and my influence with them and the rest of the associates in the facility increased significantly. As their leader, I helped the team get results.

"Leadership is a choice you make, not a place you sit." ~ John C. Maxwell

6. Connect the team when necessary.

As a leader, you have influence and connections the team doesn't. Listen and look for opportunities to speed up the process by connecting the appropriate team member with those that can and will help them. If you really want to make a high impact in this area, use your influence to get some of the right people to support the team full-time or part-time as necessary during specific projects.

As the leader, you should connect the right people at the right time for the right reason. Make it happen. It will speed up the team and ensure their success.

"Keep one degree of focus while maintaining 360 degrees of awareness. It means that we pay total attention to what is right in front of us, without losing awareness of all that is around us."
~ Robert Rabbin

7. **Cheer for the team when necessary**.

Nothing will inspire and motivate a team more than when they hear their leader cheering them on. No matter how good they may be doing, encouragement will motivate them to do better.

I remember reading about an experiment that was conducted years ago to measure people's capacity to endure pain. Psychologists measured how long a barefooted person could stand in a bucket of ice water. They found one factor made it possible for some people to stand in the freezing water twice as long as others. Can you guess what that factor was? It was encouragement.[2] As a leader, you need to harness the influential power of encouragement.

"Others know when a leader truly believes in them. Not because of what the leader says, but because of how the leader makes them feel." ~ Mack Story

8. **Give the team credit.**

High impact leaders do not want credit. They want results. They're happy to give others the credit and do so intentionally whenever they get a chance.

On all of the team events I've led, one of my goals was always to lead the team in a way that allowed them to take credit for all of the great ideas. Even if I had a part, I made sure I gave them the credit. It's never about me. It's always about them. I want them to buy-in and make it happen. That's possible when you give them credit for making things happen.

Instead of telling them what to do even when you know exactly what needs to be done, lead them by asking them questions. When they arrive at the right answer, you can give them credit for knowing exactly what to do. You will have effectively made it their idea. Always be intentional about giving credit to others.

"A candle loses nothing when it lights another candle"
~ Thomas Jefferson

9. **Take the blame for the team.**

If you want to seriously speed up the process when things go wrong, do what high impact leaders do. Step in and take the blame. Take the worry off of the team.

Too often when things go wrong or get off track, people start wasting time and energy trying to figure out who did what in an effort to place blame. This is much more prevalent in an environment where there is a lot of insecurity among low level leaders. This results in people being punished or singled out for making mistakes.

When I'm leading a team that makes a mistake, I take the blame. This allows the team to focus on the mission and why the mistake happened. If I'm the leader, I'm responsible. I should take the blame. If I don't, I'm not leading at a high level.

"When we look at people who disobey their leaders, the first question we ought to ask is not, 'What's wrong with those people?' but rather, 'What's wrong with their leader?' It says that responsibility begins at the top." ~ Malcolm Gladwell

10. Facilitate decision making with the team.

How do you know when this is necessary? It's easy. Whenever anyone asks you a question, it's necessary.

I often have leaders ask me, "How can I get my team to think for themselves?" I always say, "That's easy! Quit answering their questions." Then, I get that confused look that usually comes with a slight tilt of their head just before they say, "What do you mean quit answering their questions?" If you want your team or even your children to think for themselves, do not answer their questions.

A high impact leader knows the best answer to a question is another question. A question that causes the other person to think about the right thing. If you ask enough questions, one or both of you will learn something. Most often, both of you will learn something. In that case, your questions will be better and their answers will be better. Use questions to learn how your team thinks and to influence the right thoughts.

"The more decisions a leader makes, the further he or she is away from leading a high performance team. Make too many command decisions and you'll doom yourself and your team to mediocrity." ~ Mark Miller

These are 10 of my top tips for leading a team (influencing individuals). These principles apply in all situations with all people at all levels. They apply at work and at home. If you truly want to be a better leader, you must be able to discern what is necessary and know when it is necessary.

A high impact leader will master these principles. However, a low level leader will avoid them. If you want to lead at a high level, you must internalize these tips as habits.

Your team will not win by accident. Winning doesn't just happen. The team and the leader must intentionally and methodically find a way to win.

"By accident of fortune one may be a leader for a time, but by helping others succeed one will be a leader forever." ~ Chinese proverb

10

THE VALUE OF SIGNIFICANCE

Are you going to settle for success?

*"Significance is a choice that only
successful people can make."*
~ Mack Story

Assume you're attending your own funeral...

- **Who will you see?** Friends, family, neighbors, co-workers, leaders, followers, or strangers?
- **How many will you see?** 5, 10, 20, 50, 100, 1000, or more?
- **What are they saying?** Nothing, bad things, good things, great things, or amazing things?
- **How are they feeling?** Joyful, regretful, shameful, hopeful, grateful, or thankful?
- **What do they think of when they think of you?** Helpful, hurtful, strong, weak, happy, sad, honest, dishonest, responsible, irresponsible, head up, or head down?

Take Time for Reflection

Review the questions again. Don't cheat yourself out of this powerful, yet simple, exercise. You need to think of who you have been, who you are, and who you want to become.

Go through each question closing your eyes and thinking deeply about what you would really see and hear if you died today, at this very moment, and attended your own funeral a few days from now.

Would you have regrets about what you could have done or should have done?

I remember when I first heard Dr. Stephen R. Covey ask his audience to do a similar exercise. He was teaching "Habit 2: Begin with the End in Mind" from his book, *The 7 Habits of Highly Effective People* (my all-time favorite book by the way). While reflecting, I didn't like what I saw or what I thought. To be truthful, I didn't see much, and I didn't hear much. Why? Because I hadn't done much. At the time, I wasn't much!

I had been living my life for me. Everything was about me. I wasn't who or what I should have been at the time. That simple little exercise helped me realize I was nothing like I was making myself out to be. I wasn't just fooling everyone around me. I was fooling myself. At the time, very few people outside of my immediate family members would have attended my funeral. Very few people would have cared if I was gone, and a lot of people would have been glad. I would have left behind no legacy.

Change of Character

At the time, instead of writing a book (as I am now) on a Friday night about leadership to help other people, many I may never even meet or hear from, I would have most likely been having a drink at the local bar with some friends after a hard day at work because I thought I deserved it. Wow! Was I wasting my life away or what? I wasn't a bad person, but I wasn't even trying to live up to my potential.

I'm happy to say I've made A LOT of changes. Today, I can share with you I haven't drank alcohol or used profanity in years. I've made lots of other improvements along the way too. Dr. Covey inspired me to wake up and begin my transformation. I want to be that person for others.

The thing is, I didn't have a clue at the time. And to top it off, I thought I was successful. As a matter of fact, I was successful. I had a strong six figure income. I was always having a good time. I had a good life. I had a good wife. We had a nice home. We had nice cars. We had a lot of toys. We took a lot of vacations.

With Dr. Covey's help, I discovered what I hadn't done. I hadn't truly made a positive difference in the lives of others. I hadn't considered that I could or that I should. Sure, I was successful by most standards, but I was a long way from being significant by any standard.

At the time, I didn't know what I didn't know. But, I did know it was time to begin making changes.

"Principle-centered people are constantly educated by their experiences. They read, they seek training, they take classes, they listen to others, they learn through both their ears and eyes...they discover that the more they know, the more they realize they don't know."
~ Dr. Stephen R. Covey

My formal, personal leadership journey was about to begin. I decided I wanted to make a difference in the lives of others. As my friend, Justin Saunders, likes to say, *"Be somebody!"* That's what I wanted to do. I wanted to be somebody. The fact you're reading my second book is evidence of my unending commitment to my personal transformation and my desire to help others become more successful while hoping they will, in turn, choose to become significant and also help others. In order to do this effectively, I work on me every day. Not some days, every day. Then, I pass it on to others.

- What difference have *you* made in the lives of others? Do *you* care?
- What difference do *you* make in the lives of others? Do *you* know?
- What difference can *you* make in the lives of others? Do *you* dream?

Do you dream? This question reminds me of a story about an old Army general sitting at the bar of an officer's club staring at his third martini. A brand-new second lieutenant comes in and spots him. He can't resist sitting next to the general and starting up a conversation. The old general patiently listens to the kid and courteously answers his questions. After a time, the second lieutenant gets to what he really wants to know: "How do you make general?" he asks with raw, unconcealed ambition.

"Well son," said the old general., "here's what you do. You work like a dog, you never stop studying, you train your troops hard and take care of them. You are loyal to your commander and your soldiers. You do the best you can in every mission, and you love the Army. You are ready to die for the mission and your troops. That's all you have to do."

The second lieutenant replied with a soft, young voice, "Wow, and that's how you make general..."

"Naw!" bellowed the old general. "That's how you make first lieutenant. Just keep doing all of the things I told you and let 'em see what you've got," said the general, finishing off his last martini as he turned to walk away.[1]

The old general was saying to the young second lieutenant that in order to be successful he would need to make a career out of serving others. The general told him to start with himself. Then, train others. Then, serve everyone. Oh, and be willing to give up your life for the mission and your team if necessary. That's what serving looks like through the eyes of an old general. He basically gave a class about success and significance in just a few short sentences.

From Success to Significance

In the past, like many others, I had settled for success. Why? It was easy. It was comfortable. When I got off of work, I was through until the next day. I didn't have to worry about anything but me. I didn't have any needs or wants. Life was good. Life was simple.

However, today, things are much different. It's no longer about me. It's about we. I am never done. I am never "off work." Some people think I do what I do for the money. Sure, I want to earn money just like everyone else. But, what people don't know or don't see is I do a lot more of what I do for free than for money. I love what I do now.

I've spent many hours writing this book. That doesn't include the thousands of hours spent reading other books and filing quotes over the past years to be able to write this book. Yes, I did it for me. But, I also did it, so I could help you. It's not about me, but it starts with me.

Reading all of those books wasn't accidental. It was intentional. It would have been easier for me to continue living the life I was living before: having fun, wasting time, wasting money.....wasting my life. I had plenty of money and had plenty of fun. That's what most people are after: money and fun. But, all of my success was about me. None of my success was about you. However, this book *was* written for you.

If you're like I was, you may have never really considered the difference between a successful person and a significant person. Everyone talks about success, but hardly anyone talks about significance. People concerned only with themselves, like I used to be, are not concerned with significance. I'm hoping you already have a desire, or will develop the desire, to achieve significance in your life.

"Success is about you. Significance starts with you, but it's not about you." ~ Mack Story

Please understand there is nothing wrong with being successful. I want you to be successful. I want to help you be successful. I am not discounting success. I wish you great success! I too want to continue to be successful, but success is no longer enough for me. I want significance.

Success is vital on the journey to significance. We must first be successful before we can choose to become significant.

"While one person hesitates because he feels inferior, another person is making mistakes, and becoming superior." ~ Henry C. Link

5 Signs You Are Truly Successful

1. **You're educated.** You may or may not have a degree or two or more. Regardless of your formal education, you have a Ph.D. in results. In the real world, this is all that matters. The piece of paper some have paid for with money and time is important. However, anyone can get a degree if they are willing to do the time and pay the price. But, what you can actually do with your education is most important. You can't buy your results; you must earn them.

2. **You've climbed the ladder.** You're concerned with your own success. You've worked hard and put in the time. You've worked your way from the bottom to the top. You have arrived. You have more authority than most. You have more perks than most. You get paid more than most. You may even have a better parking spot than most.

3. **You're wealthy.** Your success can be quantified in dollars. You have the lifestyle to prove you have made some things happen. You have a big bank account. You have a fat retirement fund. You are living the life many can only dream about. You've got the fancy house, the fancy car, the fancy watch, the fancy _____.

4. **You seek comfort.** You're happy with what you have. Why wouldn't you be? You have a lot. And, you want to keep it that way. You're very comfortable and want to remain comfortable. Your goal is to maintain the status quo and coast on out the door of life. You've got what you've always wanted: you've got it made! You have paid the price for success.

5. **You're excited about retirement.** You can't wait for the day to come when you can walk away from all of your professional responsibilities forever. You track the days and count the dollars waiting for the exact moment when you can say those famous words, "Take this job and shove it. I ain't working here no more."

"People retire from a 'what,' a job. They never retire from a 'why,' their purpose." ~ Mack Story

5 Signs You Are Truly Significant

1. **You can never learn enough.** You're not focused on a degree. There is no graduation date. You're focused on a lifetime of learning and growing. You're not concerned with the generalized knowledge the masses possess. You know your passion and have found your purpose. As a result, you are laser focused on developing highly specialized knowledge in your area of giftedness.

2. **You help others climb the ladder.** Your concern has moved beyond your own success. You're now focused on the success of others. Because you're a lifetime learner with specialized knowledge, you are uniquely positioned to help others, that value what you value, climb more efficiently and effectively up the ladder of success. You are rare! Instead of selfishly hoarding knowledge, you share it intentionally with others. And, you could care less where you park.

3. **You help others become wealthy.** Not only do you help others climb the ladder of success, but you also help them become more valuable. You teach them this secret: "If you want to be a success, don't focus on becoming successful. Focus on becoming more valuable." You know true wealth does not mean having money. True wealth is having the ability to produce wealth.

4. **You seek growth.** You know real growth is a result of personal growth. You apply the 80/20 rule in this area. You spend 80% of your time working on areas of weakness relative to your character. You spend the other 20% of your time working on areas of strength relative to your competency. You know research studies have shown 87% of your results come from character and 13% come from competency. You know all of your growth happens outside your comfort zone.

5. **You never want to retire.** Because of your endless personal growth and highly developed specialized knowledge, you no longer have a career. You've found your calling, what you were put on this earth to do. You are in the zone and can no longer distinguish between work and play. It's all the same. You love what you do, and you look forward to doing it. Not just for now, but forever. The thought of retiring doesn't even cross your mind. Instead of wondering when you can retire, you wonder how long you can keep going.

"Most people don't lead their life. They accept their life." ~ John Cotter

As I continue down the path and transition from a life of success toward a life of significance, I can't help but look back at those that have been, and still are, far more successful than me still standing at the starting line refusing to take even one step toward significance. They haven't figured it out yet. They still think life is all about them and their success.

Here's my challenge to those who have already achieved success:

If you're a business owner or high level leader in an organization and have influence in regard to when and where the financial resources can be spent, be a high impact leader of significance. Invest it in the growth and development of the people that have helped make the financial resources available in the first place. Don't just train and develop the positional leaders in an effort to get better results and make the pile bigger. Go a step farther. Train and develop those on the front lines that often have the greatest potential for growth. Those that won't make it unless someone with the desire and ability reaches down and lifts them to a higher level.

If we can be that person for someone else, we should be that person for someone else. If we can and we don't, there's only one thing stopping us: our character. It's all about who we are on the inside because it shows up on the outside.

I have a tremendous passion for growing and developing not only the people at the top and in the middle, but also those people at the bottom that serve on the front lines. Why? Because I was once one of them. I was a front line factory worker, machine operator for the first 10 years of my career.

I take pride in the fact that no employer ever sent me to leadership training. I wish they would have, but they didn't. I didn't let that stop me. I found a way to make it happen! Not everyone will be self-motivated. You may be in a position to start a leadership program and include everyone at every level. If so, please consider making a real, meaningful positive impact in the life of others.

I've spent many, many thousands of my own dollars on personal growth and leadership development and many, many thousands of hours reading leadership books to be where I am today doing what I love to do: helping others. I don't simply teach these principles. I live them and apply them in my life every day. It would be a privilege and an honor to help you grow and develop through a one-on-one, professional coaching program or to help grow your team and organization with a formal, on-site leadership development training program.

You can't hold another down without staying down with them. Likewise, you can't lift another up without going up with them. Who you say you are matters. But, who you really are matters most.

Will you settle for a life of success or will you choose a life of significance?

If you travel the road to mediocrity, you will never find your *why*. However, you will find what you're willing to settle for in life. And, that's where you'll stay. If you want to find your *why*, you've got to travel the road to significance that is filled with many obstacles, setbacks, and detours along the way.

My hope is that my thoughts on the *Value of Significance* have left you reflecting on the life you're leading and the difference you have made, can make, and should be making in the lives of others in the future.

"You are not here to merely make a living. You are here in order to enable the world to live more amply, with greater vision, with a finer spirit of home and achievement. You are here to enrich the world, and you impoverish yourself if you forget the errand."
~ U.S. President, Woodrow Wilson

CONCLUSION

High impact leadership is all about creating momentum.

Momentum doesn't show up at the party alone!

My mentor, John C. Maxwell, wrote about the Law of the Big Mo in his best-selling book, The 21 Irrefutable Laws of Leadership. In it, he says, "Momentum is a leader's best friend."

I agree with John and want to end this book on values with a fun little story about momentum, "Big Mo." High impact leaders know a lot about Big Mo.

Make no mistake: Big Mo runs the show!

Know this up front: Big Mo is a party animal!! And when he shows up, he always becomes the life of the party. He likes to make things happen, so get ready to get busy when he arrives. When it comes to making Big Mo happy, if you snooze, you will definitely lose.

Big Mo needs an invitation to the party!

If you're a leader and you haven't invited Big Mo to the party, you need to put him on the top of your guest list.

There's a few more things you need to know about Big Mo. He doesn't just hang around with anyone. He never hosts his own party. And most importantly, he never travels alone.

If you're a high impact leader, rest assured, he'll be happy to come party with you. But know this, he has excellent manners and will never show up without an invitation. Without an invitation, Big Mo won't show.

If he's there and you didn't invite him, I'm here to tell you, another leader on your team did. That's okay. You should be glad you have another high impact leader on your team willing to accept the responsibility of getting Big Mo to the party.

Big Mo always travels with his team!

Everyone who has partied with Big Mo knows he doesn't show up to the party alone. Oh no, Big Mo is one of "those" guys. He *always* takes it upon himself to bring along his team.

When Big Mo arrives, don't expect him to just come right in. It'll take him a bit to get through the door. Why? Well you see, Big Mo is a really nice guy. The reason Big Mo doesn't come right in is because he's holding the door open for his team: High Speed, High Impact, High Energy, Big Advantage, Big Return, and Big Time. Don't worry. They may be a little shy at first. But once they warm up to you, it'll be like you've known them forever.

Once you have Big Mo and the team in the house, get ready!! The party is about to start! You will want to keep them there as long as possible. If they don't dig the atmosphere, they won't hesitate to make a break for the door.

"When leaders create momentum, they build upon it. They don't rest upon it." ~ Mack Story

Big Mo always designates his own host!

Think about it, every party has a host. Whenever Big Mo is on the scene, as far as he's concerned, there's only one host. It may not be the person with the formal "position" of host. Nope. Big Mo operates by his own rules. Big Mo could care less about position. Big Mo only cares about influence (leadership). Big Mo will search out the leader with the most influence and inform them they are the real host, regardless of who has the formal position.

Big Mo will then inform his team who the real host is, so they'll know who is really in charge of the party. Then, as any great servant leader would do, he lets them know as long as they are on the scene they are there to serve by helping their host make things happen. Once Big Mo has spoken and allowed the *host with the most* (influence) to take on the role as Coach (Leader/Influencer) of his team, it's really time to get the party started!

Big Mo and his team are infected and contagious!

Big Mo has an infection and is very contagious. He has already spread it to his team. They've all got it. Don't worry! Believe me, you want what they've got. They are infected with positive influence. You'll see it oozing out of them.

You must understand positive and negative influence are both contagious. You can catch either one if you get around an infected person. However, Big Mo doesn't take many chances. If you want him and his team to stick around, you must quarantine anyone infected with negative influence immediately. They must know without a doubt they are no longer welcome at the party. Big Mo and the team are not immune, and they don't want to catch a bunch of negative influence. They will pack up and leave if they find out those with negative influence are being allowed to spread it.

"When you are content with a small crowd you remain small yourself. If you live with critical people, you become critical. If you associate with negative, defeated people, then likely you will be negative and defeated also." ~ John C. Maxwell

Introduction to Big Mo's team:

Big Mo is a high impact leader. He brings out the best in his team. He knows together they bring about a synergy that isn't available when they're working alone. Magic things happen when Big Mo and his team comes to party with you and your team.

Remember, the team is contagious too. They're unleashing the power of positive influence by infecting others.

High Speed: When he's around, things happen much faster than normal. What took weeks or even months in the past, may now take just days and sometimes only hours. Those that are not infected know they will be left behind by those that are. High Speed makes sure those that aren't up to speed are being trained and developed by those that are. Those that have been infected lead with speed.

High Impact: She leaves a trail of results everywhere she goes. People that were mediocre before are now performing at levels you had only dreamed about in the past. She ensures people work together with synergy because she understands: none of us is as smart as all of us, none of us is as creative as all of us, and none of us is as strong as all of us. She makes amazing things happen in amazing ways.

High Energy: He is the one that does some pretty astonishing things. He gets those people barely able to show up on time, to show up early. He also has an ability to work with the clock watchers too. They normally can't wait for breaks, lunch, and quitting time. He works wonders with these people. They begin to be more interested in making things happen than what time it is.

Big Advantage: She changes everything. She brings a totally different perspective to the party. She has a way of putting the right people in the right place for the right reason at the right time. She has a Ph.D. in Intuition and Timing. She has a way of helping others step up and reveal their true passion and purpose. Your competition will not be happy to know she is partying with you!

Big Return: This guy is in charge of the payoff. He circles the room looking for the hidden value his fellow team members are uncovering. He understands this: no matter what the great idea is, there's always a better one. He is fully aware a better idea always means a bigger return. He always says no to the status quo. You'll always know when he's around because morale and sales will always be up.

Big Time: She's in charge of all of the fun at the party. She knows, all too well, Big Mo likes to have fun at his parties. She's in charge of celebrating the big wins and is also always acknowledging the small wins. She knows small wins add up to big wins. When she's around, there are high fives, cheering, laughing, pats on the back, and she even sometimes orders in a little pizza or ice cream to crank up the celebrations. When she leaves, Big Mo knows it's time to pack up the team and find another party.

Big Mo doesn't want the party to end!

If you want to keep Big Mo around, you've got to keep the party going. Big Mo is a party animal. He's not there because you're there. He's there because there's something going on. When the party is over, Big Mo's team will start winding down and making their way out the door.

You can always count on Big Mo closing the door behind himself with one quick look back to see if there's anyone left that still wants to party. Big Mo doesn't want to go.

"In a time of rapid change, standing still is the most dangerous course of action." ~ Brian Tracy

As a high impact leader, you are responsible for creating momentum. Don't lose track of this fact: leadership is influence. Anyone, at any time, can become the leader. Anyone can create momentum. Often to keep momentum going, you must pass the baton as relay runners do when they're competing. Don't hesitate to pass the baton when you get tired. But whatever you do, don't drop it! Keep holding on to it and keep running the race. Momentum is a leader's best friend.

If there's no momentum in your team or organization and you're the leader, it's not your team's fault. It's your fault. Whenever you place the cause of one of your actions outside of yourself, it's an excuse, not a reason.

What do you do? You get up. Join your team. And together, you start to make things happen. You invite Big Mo to the party!

High impact leaders always find a way to make it happen!

"If you want a better life personally and/or professionally, you have to ask yourself this question, 'Who am I surrounding myself with, day to day?' Those who support and create energy for change? Or those who are stuck in the comfort of what is?"
~ Dr. Henry Cloud

NOTES

Introduction
1. John C. Maxwell, *Developing the Leaders Around You: How to Help Others Reach Their Full Potential* (Nashville, TN: Thomas Nelson, 1995), 25

1. Value of Vision
1. John C. Maxwell, *Becoming a Person of Influence: How to Positively Impact the Lives of Others* (Nashville, TN: Thomas Nelson, 1995), 71

2. Value of Modeling
1. John C. Maxwell, *Today Matters: 12 Daily Practices to Guarantee Tomorrow's Success* (New York, NY: Center Street, 2004), 42

4. Value of Timing
1. John C. Maxwell, *The 15 Invaluable Laws of Growth: Live Them and Reach Your Potential* (New York, NY: Center Street, 2012), 196

5. Value of Respect
1. Author unknown

9. Value of Results
1. John C. Maxwell, *The 15 Invaluable Laws of Growth: Live Them and Reach Your Potential* (New York, NY: Center Street, 2012), 40

2. John C. Maxwell, *Becoming a Person of Influence: How to Positively Impact the Lives of Others* (Nashville, TN: Thomas Nelson, 1995), 47

10. Value of Significance
1. Colin Powell, Tony Koltz, *It Worked for Me: In Life and Leadership* (New York, NY: Harper Collins, 2012), 65

<u>FEEDBACK</u>

I would love to know what you valued most in this book, to
know your thoughts/comments, and to hear any success
stories or positive changes you may contribute to something
you learned on these pages.

mack.story@kaizenops.com

Leadership and Lean Manufacturing Support

- ✓ On-site Corporate Training: includes Mack's own fully
  customized material and 11 Learning Systems based
  on some of John Maxwell's best-selling books
- ✓ On-site Half-day/Full-day Workshops/Seminars
- ✓ Power of Effective Planning Program
- ✓ LDRSHP Boot Camp Program
- ✓ High Impact Leadership Program
- ✓ High Impact Chamber Program
- ✓ High Impact Marketing Program
- ✓ Individual and Team Coaching
- ✓ Individual and Team Mentoring
- ✓ On-site or Virtual Mastermind Groups
- ✓ Keynote Speech for Your Company Sponsored Event
- ✓ Executive and Personal Retreats
- ✓ Partnership Summits
- ✓ On-site Lean Leadership Certification
- ✓ On-site Lean Manufacturing Certification
- ✓ On-site Lean Manufacturing Event Facilitation
- ✓ On-site Lean Manufacturing Training

For more information please visit:
www.mackstory.com
www.linkedin.com/in/mackstory
www.achieveabundantlife.com

ABOUT THE AUTHOR

Mack's journey is filled with personal and professional growth. He married Ria in 2001. He has one son, Eric, born in 1991.

After graduating from high school in 1987, Mack joined the United States Marine Corps Reserve as a 0311 infantryman. Soon after in 1988, he began his 20 plus year career in manufacturing on the front lines of a production machine shop. Graduating with highest honors, he earned an Executive Bachelor of Business Administration degree from Faulkner University in 2002.

He found his niche in lean manufacturing and, along with it, developed his passion for leadership. In 2008, he launched, KaizenOps, a Lean Manufacturing and Leadership Development Consulting Company.

Mack is a John Maxwell Team Certified Leadership Coach, Trainer, and Speaker. John C. Maxwell is one of the world's most recognized leadership experts. John has written nearly 80 books and has trained millions in many countries worldwide.

Mack's experience with the John Maxwell Team includes teaching, speaking, coaching, and an international training event as part of the Cultural Transformation in Guatemala where over 20,000 leaders were trained in one week.

Mack has shared the stage with his mentor Les Brown, an international motivational speaker. Les was selected one of America's Top Five Speakers for 1992 by Toastmasters international.

Mack is an inspiration for people everywhere as an example of achievement, growth, and personal development. His passion inspires people all over the world! He believes everything rises and falls on influence.

Defining Influence
by Mack Story

In *Defining Influence*, I outline the foundational leadership principles and lessons we must learn in order to develop our character in a way that allows us to increase our influence with others. I also share many of my personal stories revealing how I got it wrong many times in the past and how I grew from front-line factory worker to become a Leadership Expert.

I wrote *Defining Influence* to help answer these questions:

1. ***Why*** **do we influence?** – Our character determines *why* we influence. Who we are on the inside is what matters. Do we manipulate or motivate? It's all about intent.

2. ***How*** **do we influence?** – Our character, combined with our competency, determines *how* we influence. Who we are and what we know combine to create our unique style of influence which determines our methods of influence.

3. ***Where*** **do we influence?** – Our passion and purpose determine *where* we have the greatest influence. What motivates and inspires us gives us the energy and authenticity to motivate and inspire others.

4. ***Who*** **do we influence?** – We influence those *who* buy-in to us. Only those valuing and seeking what we value and seek will volunteer to follow us. They give us or deny us permission to influence them based on how well we have developed our character and competency.

5. ***When*** **do we influence?** – We influence others *when* they want our influence. We choose when others influence us. Everyone else has the same choice. They decide when to accept or reject our influence. We only influence others when they want to change.

Available on Amazon.com in paperback and eBook.
Or, order your signed copy at www.mackstory.com.

Excerpt from *Defining Influence*:

INTRODUCTION

"Leadership is influence. Nothing more. Nothing less.
Everything rises and falls on leadership."
~ John C. Maxwell

Everyone is born a leader.

I haven't always believed everyone is a leader. You may or may not at this point. That's okay. There is a lot to learn about leadership.

At this very moment, you may already be thinking to yourself, "I'm not a leader." My goal is to help you understand why everyone is a leader and to help you develop a deeper understanding of the principles of leadership and influence.

Developing a deep understanding of leadership, has changed my life for the better. It has also changed the lives of my family members, friends, associates, and clients. I want to help you improve not only your life, but also the lives of those around you.

Until I became a student of leadership which eventually led me to become a John Maxwell Team Certified Leadership Coach, Trainer, and Speaker, and author, I did not understand leadership or realize everyone can benefit from learning the related principles.

In the past, I thought leadership was a term associated with being the boss and having formal authority over others. Those people are definitely leaders. But, I had been missing something. All of the other seven billion people on the planet are leaders too.

Why do I say everyone is born a leader? I agree with John Maxwell, "Leadership is Influence. Nothing more. Nothing less." Everyone has influence. It's a fact. Therefore, everyone is a leader.

No matter your age, gender, religion, race, nationality, location, or position, everyone has influence. Whether you want to be a leader or not, you are. After reading this book, I hope you do not question whether or not you are a leader. However, I do hope you question what type of leader you are and what level leader you are.

Everyone does not have authority, but everyone does have influence. There are plenty of examples in the world of people without authority leading people through influence alone. Actually, every one of us is an example. We have already done it. We know it is true. This principle is self-evident which means it contains its own evidence and does not need to be demonstrated or explained; it is obvious to everyone.

The question to ask is not, "Are you a leader?" The question is, "What type of leader are you?" The answer: whatever kind you choose to be. Choosing not to be a leader is not an option. As long as you live, you will have influence. You are a leader.

You had influence before you were born and may have influence after your death. How? Thomas Edison still influences the world every time a light is turned on, you may do things in your life to influence others long after you're gone. Or, you may pass away with few people noticing. It depends on the choices you make.

Even when you're alone, you have influence. The most important person you will ever influence is yourself. The degree to which you influence yourself determines the level of influence you ultimately have with others. Typically, when we are talking about leading ourselves, the word most commonly used to describe self-leadership is discipline which can be defined as giving yourself a command and following through with it. We must practice discipline daily to increase our influence with others. It is not something we do only when we feel like it.

"We must all suffer one of two things: the pain of discipline or the pain of regret or disappointment."
~ Jim Rohn

As I define leadership as influence, keep in mind the word leadership and influence can be interchanged anytime and anyplace. They are one and the same. Throughout this book, I'll help you remember by placing one of the words in parentheses next to the other occasionally as a reminder. They are synonyms. When you read one, think of the other.

Everything rises and falls on influence (leadership). When you share what you're learning, clearly define leadership as influence for others. They need to understand the context of what you are teaching and understand they *are* leaders (people with influence) too. If you truly want to learn and apply leadership principles, you must start teaching this material to others within 24-48 hours of learning it yourself.

You will learn the foundational principles of leadership (influence) which will help you understand the importance of the following five questions. You will be able to take effective action by growing yourself and possibly others to a higher level of leadership (influence). Everything you ever achieve, internally and externally, will be a direct result of your influence.

1. ***Why* do we influence?** – Our character determines *why* we influence. Who we are on the inside is what matters. Do we manipulate or motivate? It's all about intent.

2. ***How* do we influence?** – Our character, combined with our competency, determines *how* we influence. Who we are and what we know combine to create our unique style of influence which determines our methods of influence.

3. ***Where* do we influence?** – Our passion and purpose determine *where* we have the greatest influence. What motivates and inspires us gives us the energy and authenticity to motivate and inspire others.

4. ***Who* do we influence?** – We influence those *who* buy-in to us. Only those valuing and seeking what we value and seek will volunteer to follow us. They give us or deny us permission to influence them based on how well we have developed our character and competency.

5. ***When* do we influence?** – We influence others *when* they want our influence. We choose when others influence us. Everyone else has the same choice. They decide when to accept or reject our influence. We only influence others when they want to change.

The first three questions are about the choices we make as we lead (influence) ourselves and others. The last two questions deal more with the choices others will make as they decide first, *if* they will follow us, and second, *when* they will follow us. They will base their choices on *who we are* and *what we know*.

Asking these questions is important. Knowing the answers is more important. But, taking action based on the answers is most important. Cumulatively, the answers to these questions determine our leadership style and our level of influence (leadership).

On a scale of 1-10, your influence can be very low level (1) to very high level (10). But make no mistake, you *are* a leader. You *are* always on the scale. The higher on the scale you are the more effective you are. You will be at different levels with different people at different times depending on many different variables.

Someone thinking they are not a leader or someone that doesn't want to be a leader, is still a leader. They will simply remain a low level leader with low level influence getting low level results. They will likely spend much time frustrated with many areas of their life. Although they could influence a change, they choose instead to be primarily influenced by others.

What separates higher level leaders from lower level leaders? There are many things, but two primary differences are:

1) Higher level leaders accept more responsibility in all areas of their lives while lower level leaders tend to blame others and transfer responsibility more often.

2) Higher level leaders have more positive influence while lower level leaders tend to have more negative influence.

My passion has led me to grow into my purpose which is to help others increase their influence personally and professionally while setting and reaching their goals. I am very passionate and have great conviction. I have realized many benefits by getting better results in all areas of my life. I have improved relationships with my family members, my friends, my associates, my peers, and my clients. I have witnessed people within these same groups embrace leadership principles and reap the same benefits.

The degree to which I *live* what I teach determines my effectiveness. My goal is to learn it, live it, and *then* teach it. I had major internal struggles as I grew my way to where I am. I'm a long way from perfect, so I seek daily improvement. Too often, I see people teaching leadership but not living what they're teaching. If I teach it, I apply it.

My goal is to be a better leader tomorrow than I am today. I simply have to get out of my own way and lead. I must lead me effectively before I can lead others effectively, not only with acquired knowledge, but also with experience from applying and living the principles.

I'll be transparent with personal stories to help you see how I have applied leadership principles by sharing: How I've struggled. How I've learned. How I've sacrificed. How I've succeeded.

Go beyond highlighting or underlining key points. Take the time to write down your thoughts related to the principle. Write down what you want to change. Write down how you can apply the principle in your life. You may want to consider getting a journal to fully capture your thoughts as you progress through the chapters. What you are thinking as you read is often much more important than what you're reading.

Most importantly, do not focus your thoughts on others. Yes, they need it too. We all need it. I need it. You need it. If you focus outside of yourself, you are missing the very point. Your influence comes from within. Your influence rises and falls based on your choices. You have untapped and unlimited potential waiting to be released. Only you can release it.

You, like everyone else, were born a leader. Let's take a leadership journey together.

(If you enjoyed this Introduction to *Defining Influence*, it is available in paperback and as an eBook on Amazon.com or for a signed paperback copy you can purchase at mackstory.com.)

Ria's Story: From Ashes to Beauty
by Ria Story

The unforgettable story and inspirational memoir of a young woman who was sexually abused by her father from age 12 – 19 and then rejected by her mother.

For the first time, Ria publicly reveals details of the sexual abuse she endured growing up. 13 years after leaving home at 19, she decided to speak out about her story and encourage others to find hope and healing.

Determined to not only survive, but also thrive, Ria shares how she was able to overcome the odds and find hope and healing to Achieve Abundant Life. She shares the leadership principles that she applied to find professional success, personal significance, and details how she was able to find the courage to share her story to give hope to others around the world.

Ria states, "It would be easier for me to let this story go untold forever and simply move on with life… One of the most difficult things I've ever done is write this book. Victims of sexual assault or abuse don't want to talk because they want to avoid the social stigma and the fear of not being believed or the possibility of being blamed for something that was not their fault. My hope and prayer is that someone will benefit from learning how I was able to overcome such difficult circumstances. That brings purpose to the pain and reason enough to share what I would rather have left behind forever. Our scars make us stronger."

Available at Amazon.com in paperback and eBook.

To order your signed copy, to learn more about Ria, or to book her to speak at your event, please visit her website:

www.achieveabundantlife.com

A.C.H.I.E.V.E. – *7 Keys to Unlock Success, Significance, and Your Potential*
by Ria Story

We all have hopes, dreams, and goals that we want to ACHIEVE. Unfortunately, how to ACHIEVE isn't taught in school or college.

This tip book shares 7 lessons and short stories on: **A**ttitude, **C**hoices, **H**umility, **I**ntegrity, **E**nergy, **V**ision, and **E**xcellence.

Ria's story is one of faith, hope, love, and inspiration. She left home at 19, after years of sexual abuse, with no job, no money, and no high school diploma. What she did have was faith. She found a job as a waitress and started working to earn her GED, so she could later attend college where she earned an MBA graduating with a 4.0 GPA.

Ria is certified as a John Maxwell Leadership Coach, Trainer and Speaker. John C. Maxwell is one of the world's most recognized leadership experts. John has written nearly 80 books and has trained millions worldwide.

Ria's experience with the John Maxwell Team includes teaching, speaking, coaching, and an international training event as part of the Transformation in Guatemala. Ria offers performance coaching, inspirational speaking, and leadership development services.

Website: www.achieveabundantlife.com
LinkedIn: www.linkedin.com/riastory
Twitter: www.twitter.com/Ria_Story
Facebook:
www.facebook.com/Ria.Story.Speaker.Coach.Trainer